Published by mjwindsorpublishingllc

mjwindsor.com

ISBN: 9798330562251

Cover design by M. J. Windsor

PROLOGUE

The road down to the cemetery was full of spring blooms and bright, green leaves waving in the gentle breeze that was coming in through the open car window. The old station wagon rumbled down the gravel road, playing disco music through its speakers, but the bright music did nothing to brighten the spirits of the three occupants.

Charles Defaid watched out the window as the cemetery came closer. He could hear his mother, Emma, quietly sniffling next to him. He held her hand and gave it a gentle squeeze as they drove past the entrance. At 20 years old, he couldn't believe his father was gone. He had been such a strong, vital person. It didn't make sense that he was taken away from them by a small sickness, such as pneumonia.

Stepping out of the wagon, he joined his Great Aunt Josie and their friends from church at the grave site. His mother hung off him, nearly inconsolable. Aunt Josie handed her a tissue, and smiled softly to her, taking her hand and leading her to the grave.

The service was short, and many people gave condolences, but it was bittersweet. The wake was to be held at his family home with everybody bringing a dish to pass and celebrating the life of a good man.

Evening came on slowly and the lights of the house shone out into the yard where the old house once stood but was now a family gathering place. Charles walked over to the picnic table and sat, staring at the night sky. His Aunt Josie slowly crossed the pathway toward him, carrying a book in her hands. She sat down, waving off his helping hands. "I'm not too old to find my own way yet, young Charles," she said, smiling. She set the book, he could see it was an old journal, on the table and tapped it with her index finger.

"What is that, Aunt Josie?" asked Charles.

"This, my child, is the Defaid family journal, which was passed down to me as the oldest in the family. With the sudden passing of your father, it now goes to you, once I have passed. There is much that we need to discuss before the night is over," said Aunt Josie.

Aunt Josie opened the journal to the pages that talked about the historical family fire that destroyed their old farmhouse in 1870. "Pieces of the first Defaid family

journal were able to be saved from that fire, but most of the stories passed down since are mere remembrances," she says, laying the old journal on the table in front of Charles, "It is our task to keep these stories, these family secrets, for future generations, Charles. We must not fail!"

Charles picks up the journal and sees that some of the information is in Welsh, the tongue of the ancestors. Surprised, he reads the journal and feels himself flush with anxiety. "But, Aunt Josie, I don't understand! Why am I being told this now? You said these things happened many years ago. What does that have to do with me now? Why would anyone come all the way from Wales to harm us? This is Canada, Aunt Josie, were just farmers trying to live a good life. We've never hurt anyone," says Charles.

"Young Charles, I'm truly sorry you're the one who has to carry this burden. You have so many years ahead of you, and I should be passing this onto your Grampa Percival, God rest his soul, and he in turn passing it onto your father, but fate didn't see it that way. Now you will hold this story to your heart until your time comes or, heaven forbid, they return. If they were to return it is then, and only then, shall you reveal to our bloodline this tale I have laid upon you. Do you understand?" says Aunt Josie.

"Yes Ma'am, I understand," says Charles.

"I know you Charles and your heart is pure," Aunt Josie says, smiling at the young man.

"Aunt Josie, how long have you had to carry this secret?" asks Charles.

"I was fifteen years old in 1900 when my father died of a stroke. Your Grampa Percival was just five at the time, and because I was the oldest of our bloodline I carried the secret. You will be the oldest of the bloodline soon, after I have passed on," said Aunt Josie.

"Eighty years, Aunt Josie. That's a long time to keep a secret," says Charles.

"Yes, and so is ninety-five, young man. Now, be off with you and always remember you are never alone or without aid, even when I am gone, the spirits of our family will guide you," she says.

CHAPTER ONE

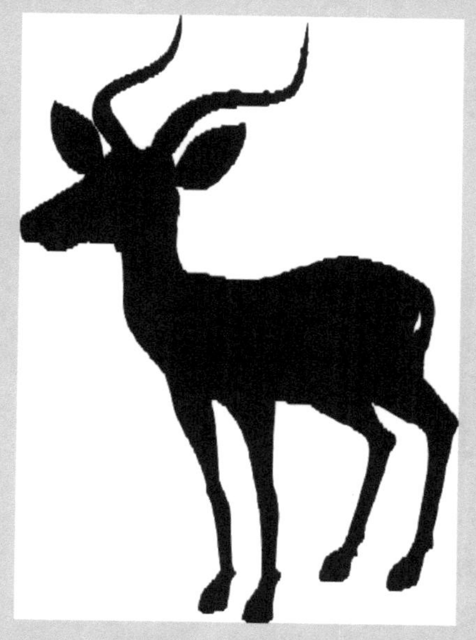

“What do you say we go for a walk Kay? It’s a beautiful day. The birds are singing, and the bees are buzzing. It’s a great morning. We can head up to the lake and say hi to Grand Daddy,” says Ken.

Kay wagged her tail and pranced with anticipation, prancing around him as he walked toward the northern part of the property. She loved to swim in the lake and chase after the frogs. Ken always thought that a bit strange for a Border Collie, but they didn’t mind. If his best buddy was happy then so was he.

He liked to fish on the far northwest side of Lake Percival where there’s more shade and a nice comfortable spot to sit and relax. Following the path north around the west side of the lake he reaches his resting place and takes a seat on his favorite stump. Now this isn’t any run of the mill stump; its what’s left of a very large oak tree that fell many years ago.

Grampa Charles said he found it when he was a boy on his first trip to the lake with his friends when he was 12 years old. At that time a hollow trunk was all that remained, but it was huge! As Grampa Charles puts it, “the Grand Daddy of the forest,” and it stood a good twelve feet tall, and about eight feet across at the base. He loved that old tree. For many years he would make it his go to friend, his best friend. There came a time, though, when a hard choice had to be made. It seemed that Grand Daddy of the forest was about to split right down the middle. After all those years with his friend, he had to take it down. He worried over it for quite some time. Finally, one day he was standing near his old friend, with tears filling his eyes. With his saw in hand, he touched and patted his companion. Then from out of nowhere, a thought came to him, he shouted out, “You’ll become a throne my old friend. A mighty seat fit for the lord of the forest.”

Charles trimmed off the upper shell of the hallowed old tree stump till only a five-foot section remained. He cleared out the inside, taking out old birds’ nests and damp leaves from last season’s fall, and from his families barn he found two large flat boards which he placed in the stump as a bench with a back rest. He looked around for a base to support the seat of the throne and found two large square boulders he could drag from the lake shore and placed them inside the tree stump.

Now the tree which once was a child’s hideaway, a realm where dreams came true and battles were fought and won, and a boy became a man, serves as a throne. A symbol of strength and a place for respite for any who wish to rest; a place of comfort and a listener for any dreamer who wishes to stay for a while. Sitting there always reminded Ken of when Grampa Charles would tell the story of the

“Grand Daddy of the forest.’ He never grew tired of hearing that tale. He loved to watch as his grandfather gestured with his hands and recreated the height of the old stump, and how his eyes would sparkle with joy as he reminisced about the adventures he had playing there as a boy.

Ken sat listening to the birds singing and watched a few herons out on the edge of the lake catch fish with their long beaks, and relaxed into the day, no worries on the horizon. Kay sat next to him and kept busy keeping a watchful eye out for any frogs, ready to pounce if one should be brave enough to appear. The cardinals were easy to recognize, as was the owl as it called to its partner. He enjoyed just listening to nature while sitting within Grampa Charles’ throne, cozy within its wooden arms. He heard the short chirp of the cardinal’s alarmed call, and he sensed that something wasn’t right. The cardinals fluttered off from the tree branch they were building a nest on, and the owl, with wings stretched out, floated silently over the lake to its south side and vanished into the leaf covered branches of a tall maple. Kay’s eye followed the owl until it vanished and then she turned her head and looked up at Ken, her tongue lolling. She settled down at his feet, muzzle resting on Ken’s feet, waiting for his next move.

His senses were on high alert as he got to his feet. Slowly, he scanned his surroundings. Taking in the silence that suddenly hung over the lake shore. The frogs had gone silent, and the heron could be seen flying slowly away to the east side of the lake. It was an eerie feeling, the sudden silence, and being alone on the lake didn’t seem like the safest place to be right at that moment. He bent down and patted Kay’s head reassuringly, but he was not sure who he was trying to calm, himself or the dog.

Then from behind him he picked up a faint sound. Something big was running through the brush. The sound became louder the closer it came. Instinctively, he dropped to one knee. Putting his arm around Kay to keep her in place, he tried to see into the dense forest as he peered to the north over Grand Daddy. Then a large buck emerged from a thicket and stopped not twenty paces from him. Its eyes were opened wide with fear and its breathing was labored as blood spewed from its mouth. Ken watched as it took its last breath and fell to the forest’s floor.

Ken remained inside Grand Daddy for several minutes waiting of any movement, but there was no movement coming from where the deer exited the forest. Finally, Ken’s all clear came when the birds returned to the trees and began their normal chattering noises. No one had come to claim their kill, and that upset him.

He released his hold on Kay, and walked slowly to where the deer lay, scanning his surroundings. A beautiful ten-point buck rested at his feet. Kay whined as she sniffed the fallen buck.

“Why would anyone take your life for no good reason?” asked Ken.

Ken knelt down to inspect the wound. This wasn’t a new scene for him, but he was surprised to see the cause of death had been by crossbow. Its feathers were covered in blood, but he could see the red and black fletching colors through the redness as he pulled the bolt from the deer. At first it wasn’t noticeable, being covered in blood, but after a closer inspection he could see this was no ordinary bolt.

“Dad and Grampa Charles will need to see this.”

The crossbow was Ken’s favorite for hunting deer. Every fall since he was thirteen, he would go out and bring back a deer for the family to enjoy. He used his dad’s crossbow till his sixteenth birthday when his Grampa Charles presented him with his own. Now his old one was displayed on the wall in the family room next to his dads and Grandpa Charles’s. A carved wooden plaque hung above them which read, ‘Byth Heb’ that in Welsh meant, ‘Never Without.’

Ken found a blood trail and followed it back into the woods until he came to Dee Run, the stream that feeds into Lake Percival. He went to the west side and found no sign of a blood trail. He searched upstream for about a hundred yards, but there was nothing to show that a large deer had passed through this way. He stood by the stream scanning the surrounding forest, looking if he could see where the deer had broken through. It had to have come this way when it made its way toward the lake. He turned around and ran back down the path, following the worn trail back toward Grand Daddy.

It was getting warmer, and he had to get the deer back to the farm soon. Crossing back over the stream, he was startled when a cardinal flew in front of him. Ken watched as it landed on a nearby tree calling a warning tune out to him. He felt that he wasn’t alone, and he crouched down, grabbing on to Kay’s collar, as he looked through the trees to see if he could spy anyone around. When nothing moved, he looked up at the Cardinal, who was still perched upon the tree limb.

“You gotta be kidding me,” muttered Ken. He couldn’t believe what he was looking at. The bird was perched on a bolt. Ken stood there in a daze, unsure of reality, the bolt was stuck six feet up the tree, the same black and red fletching as the one in the deer. Finally, the bird flew off when he moved in to take a closer look, giving him an annoyed chirp. Taking the first bolt from his pocket, he compared them. Both looked the same, but of a type he wasn't familiar with, wooden, almost homemade; not the aluminum alloy construction makes, like the ones his family uses. He then looked down the shafts length and followed it into the area it had traveled through.

"They must have been pretty close. There's not a way they got a shot through all those trees. Come on, Kay. We have got get back home. Dad and Grampa will not be happy that we have a poacher on our land again."

Pulling it out of the tree required a lot of tugging, but he got it out after a few pulls. The shaft and tip came away without damage, but the tip was bent slightly, which could only mean that his assumption was correct, it had been a close shot.

Returning to the fallen deer, Ken cleared the area it had fallen near and got it field stripped. He then gathered his fishing gear and returned to the farm to bring back the Panther, the farm's side-by-side. Any further investigation of the area would have to wait. Getting the deer's remains home was his top priority.

CHAPTER TWO

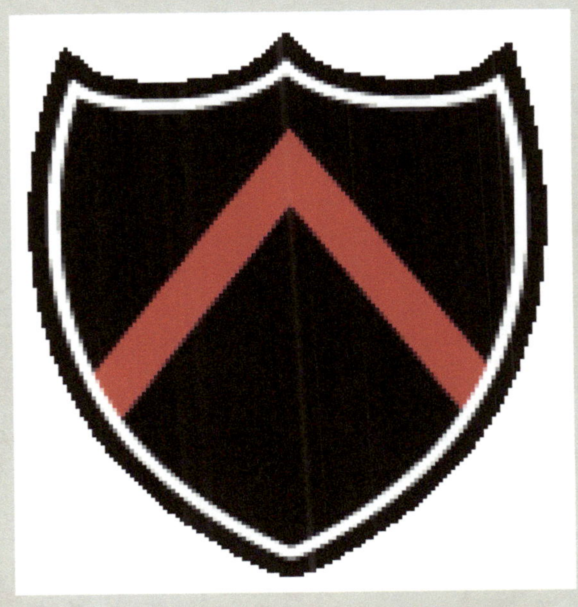

“All done, Mom,” shouted Griffin, who came running from around the chicken coop. “I’ll be in my room if you need me.”

“Hold on there, Mister,” said his mother, Amelia, a tall, blond woman about forty, but who could pass for twenty-five, “you didn’t clean the chicken coop yesterday. I know you know what the rules are. Go on, Mister, clean out the coop, then you can play on your tablet.”

Griffin, Ken’s twelve-year-old brother, would rather be playing shooter video games on his tablet than doing chores. He’ll be thirteen this August and in September he’ll be strapped with Ken’s chores as well when he leaves for college.

“But Mom…,” cried Griffin, feeling very put upon, and not happy that chores took him away from his fun. “Owen is waiting for me! We have a campaign to finish. The second realm elves are going to destroy the enemies of the Razen.”

Amelia could see how excited he was. It was all he could talk about for days. With summer vacation starting, Griffin and his friend Owen had been completely absorbed in the actions of the video game they started playing a few weeks ago.

“No buts Griff. It’ll only take twenty minutes at the most. Now get to it!” said his mother sternly, shooing him toward the chicken coops.

Amelia smiled as she watched Griff turn toward the chicken coop. She knew his heart wasn’t into farming, but he always did as he was told even if it took a little persuasion at times. She watched him for a few minutes as he grumpily opened the coop and grabbed the rake, starting to gather all the used hay into a pile for the mulch pile. The chickens pecked the ground around him happy at the chance to catch a stray kernel of food.

Finished with her weeding, Amelia hung the hoe in the shed and went to the house for a breather on the porch swing. Sitting down she gently started the swing moving with a nudge of her foot. She thought of Griffin having to pick up on Ken’s chores while he was away at college. She couldn’t believe her little boy, so happy and carefree, was old enough to leave home and go off to college.

Her mind drifted back four years ago when Gwen got married to Sayer and left for the city. Ken was fourteen and had to pick up his sister’s chores. She remembers his delight in feeding the sheep, and tending to the rose bushes, especially those by the mailbox, put a smile on her face. Once a week, when the roses were in bloom, he would put a rose in the box for Mrs. Plotts, the rural mail carrier. He had a bit of a crush on that pretty young lady, and she always waved to him when

she dropped off the mail and came by with a package. Tragically, she got married to a nice man at the county sheriff's office, and Ken had been heartbroken.

"All done, Mom," says Griffin as he comes up the porch steps. The swing moved back and forth as he sat next to her. She ruffled his hair a bit, laughing when he stuck his tongue out at her in response.

"Have you seen your brother since breakfast?" asked Amelia.

"He and Kay were headed up the trail. Looked like they were gonna go fishing; he had his fishing stuff with him," says Griffin.

"Oh, yeah, he did mention something about that at supper last night," says Amelia.

"Well, he better have got his chores done cause I ain't gonna do them," grumps Griffin, as he jumps of the swing and heads toward the front door.

"Griffin Defaid!" exclaimed Amelia. "I know you're not happy that Ken is leaving in the fall for college, but you shouldn't be giving any of us an attitude just because you're upset about it."

Griffin abruptly stopped and turned to face his mother, "Sorry, Mom," he mumbled.

Amelia's stern demeanor slowly turned into a smile, "I love you, Griffin."

Griffin returned her smile, "love you too Mom!" he said, and spun around running into the house. She sat back and closed her eyes letting the sway of the swing lull her into a relaxing state. Sitting down on the steps of the porch next to Amelia, her husband, Gavin, took in her relaxed features and smiled, happy that the farm was doing well after a hard winter.

"Say there, young lady, can I have a seat next to you?" asked Gavin.

"Yes, you may, young man. Here's a special seat just for you," says Amelia, smiling. Without opening her eyes, she patted the spot on the swing closest to her. He shuffled over to be closer to her and asked, "How's your morning been, Hun?" He took the seat and wrapped his arm around her shoulders.

"Well, let me think about that for a minute," said Amelia. Eyes still closed; she placed her head on his shoulder.

“Oh-oh, what did Griff do this time?” Gavin playfully asked.

“You mean your youngest son? Your, soon to be, right hand man?” she asked. “All he wants to do is stay in his room playing on that tablet or running around the property looking for imaginary adventures. He’s not really interested in the farm you know, Gavin” sighing, she played with the fingers of their hands, wrapping them together and giving them a squeeze.

“He’ll come around, Hun. It takes a little longer with some and not every day does someone come around that has Kenrich’s love of farming,” Gavin says, trying to sooth Amelia’s frustration at the indifference Griffin has to farming. “Ken loves the animals and the lands, it’s just who he is, but Griff is a different animal altogether, and he is only 12, can’t expect too much from him yet.”

“Yeah, I know. I guess I’m just not ready to lose another one so soon. You know what it was like for us when Gwen married Sayer, and now Ken’s leaving for college in September,” laments Amelia, thinking about how quiet the house will be with two of the three children borne their being gone from the house.

“Yeah, I know, Hun, but Gwen’s happy and we can relax knowing how good a husband and father Sayer has become. He works so hard to provide for them,” Gavin says.

“He sure lives up to being Welsh, name and all,” Amelia says.

“You said it! He’s got some fine carpentry skills. It shows in that shed he built for us from that pile of lumber left over when the old barn finally collapsed during that storm, we had this last March,” says Gavin.

“Well, here comes our college boy now. I guess we won’t be having fish for supper,” jokes Amelia, seeing Ken is without the fish he promised to catch for dinner.

“No fish Mom, but venison might be on the menu if I can find the Panther with its cart to load up the deer. It’s not in the barn, Dad. Did Griff take off to the Woodson’s with it?” asked a flushed looking Ken.

“Grampa Charles has it out on the east pasture checking fence lines,” says Amelia.

“Did I hear you say venison? It’s July son, too soon to be taking deer,” asked his father, curiously.

“I know Dad, I would never take a deer out of season!” says Ken.

“Your father wasn’t accusing you, Ken,” says Amelia, placatingly. “We all know you know that this isn’t the season to take a deer,” says Amelia.

“Yeah, I know. I guess I’m upset about the deer too. Sorry Dad,” Ken says, blushing.

“No worry, now tell us how you came across this deer,” says Gavin.

“It came to me, Dad, well to us,” he says, looking down at his dog, Kay.

“Where did you find it at then?” asked Amelia.

“We were sitting in Grand Daddy, and I hadn’t even thrown out a line yet, when I heard it running through the forest. It stopped and dropped near us,” says Ken, excitedly.

“Did you hear any shot!” inquires Gavin.

“There were no shots, at least not from a rifle,” says Ken, holding out the two crossbow bolts to is father for investigation.

“Let’s have a look,” Gavin says. He stands up and steps down the porch steps, and taking the bolts from Ken, he inspects them closely, running a finger over the soft feathers of the fletching.

“I’ve never seen this type of bolt before, Dad,” says Ken, “it looks almost homemade, not the normal bolt we use.”

“Neither have I, maybe your Grampa Charles can help us with that,” says Gavin, curious to see if Charles will be able to shed some light on the origins of the mystery bolts. His knowledge about hunting is more advanced than his own.

CHAPTER THREE

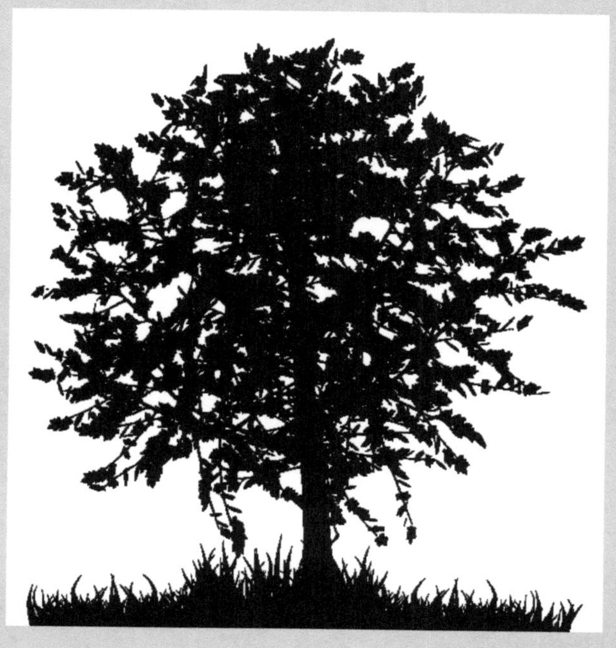

Grampa Charles decided to give Griff a break and check the fence lines himself. Actually, he likes riding the Panther, and since it was just sitting in the shed, he figured this would be a good time for a ride.

The Dafaid farm was quite large, and Griffin had been given the chore of checking the north fence line a few weeks ago. The three hundred tillable acres in the lowlands, and a hundred or so acres full of rocky outcrops and grassy plains for grazing the farm's many cattle and sheep. Beyond that was the valley, filled with forests and streams, wooded and too steep to work from, the home of Lake Percival, and a pain to bring the cattle and sheep through.

Lake Percival was in the valley, in the northern part of the property, and that's where Charles was really wanting to go. He's been planning to take a trip up there for a visit to his old friend, Grand Daddy, the throne of the forest. He had stopped the cart at the far northeast corner of the pasture. A small tree limb had fallen on the fence and knocked the barbed wire loose on a corner post.

"Ok, where'd that thing go to?" said Charles, looking for his hammer. "I'm gonna have to tie the darn hammer down, disappearing every time I need it!" He got off the Panther and checked the back of the cart. Swearing lightly, he picked up his hammer and stuck it through the belt loop of his pants. The limb lay over the fence, bending it and twisting the wire around the branch. The corner support was the only thing keeping that section of fence from collapsing. He quickly untangled the limb from the wire and threw it into the trees nearby. As he turned to mend the wire, something on the fence caught his attention.

"What the heck! Is that some kind of drawing?" asked Charles, upon seeing a strange brand or drawing on the fence post nearest to him. It wasn't a very neat drawing, more like it was drawn in haste. He had to get pretty close to make out the details of it. It was a shield, black in color, except for a red chevron running straight through the middle of it. The red color was what had initially caught him off-guard.

"Oh no, this can't be! What the hell is going on here?" puzzled, Charles reached over to the fence and touched the still tacky red paint. "Wait a minute. I think I know who'd done this and I think it's time Griffin and I have a little talk." He reattached the broken wire with a sure strike of his hammer and checked the posts nearby. All were in good shape with no loose wires, and more importantly, no more mysterious drawings. With his mind at ease, even with a mystery to solve, he took the Panther further along the fence line toward the north gate. On the gates top frame was another drawing similar to the one he found earlier, but larger and

created with a steadier hand.

"What the…!" exclaimed Charles. He reached in his pocket and pulled out his phone, which was more of a stranger to him than his toothbrush.

"This thing's a pain in my side, too small, how is anybody supposed to punch in these numbers? Darn it, I'll get a hold of Gavin when I get back home," says Charles, shoving the phone back into his back pocket. Getting back on the Panther and before he could start its engine, his phone vibrated.

"Ok, now what?" he says, already irritated with the marking on the fence and now his phone.

His patience was getting a bit thin as he shut off the vehicle and stepped off. He could feel a vibration and hear a ring incessantly coming from his pocket. Pulling it out, he answered the phone gruffly.

"Hello," says Charles, in an unfriendly tone.

"Wow Dad, you, OK?" asks Gavin, his normally jovial father wasn't known to be so grumpy.

"Oh…Hi Gavin. Sorry, no, I mean yeah, I'm OK. It's this damn phone gadget, my fingers are too big for the little buttons. There are also some strange markings on the fence line. They've gotten me a bit flustered."

"OK, will you be back soon? Ken needs the Panther right away," asks Gavin, trying not to let his humor leak into his voice at his father's mood.

"I'm headed that way now. We need to have a talk with Griffin when I get back," says Charles.

"About what, Dad?" asks Gavin.

"Something I found when I checked the fence. I'll tell you when I get home," says Charles.

"OK. Oh, and Dad, be nice to your phone," teases Gavin before hanging up.

"Yeah, right!" says Charles, as he used a little extra force to close his phone. Hurrying back to the house he hopes everything was ok with Ken. It wasn't like him to return so early from fishing, usually he's not seen until evening chores.

Gavin and Ken were standing by the shed when Charles showed up with the Panther.

"What brought you back so early, Ken?" says Charles.

"Someone has downed a big buck up by Grand Daddy. I want to get up there as soon as possible," says Ken.

"Who the heck's been hunting on our land out of season?" asks Charles, forehead wrinkling as he squints his blue eyes in anger.

"That was my thought too, Dad," says Gavin.

"Well, you better get back up their Ken, it's getting warmer by the minute," says Charles grumbles as he climbs off of the Panther.

"I'm going with him, Dad. He's gonna need some help getting the deer loaded. While we're out, take a look at these bolts Ken found," says Gavin, handing the bolts to his father.

"One was in the deer and the other I found in a tree. Here's the point for that one Grampa,' says Ken, showing Charles the snapped off bolt point.

"We'll be back soon," says Gavin.

Ken pointed at the ground and looked at Kay, the dog whined a bit, but settled to the ground near Charles feet. Ken started the Panther and drove off. Charles watch as Gavin and Ken went around the barn, and out of sight. He looked down at the two bolts in his hand.

"Hunting with a crossbow and out of season too. I'm gonna call the game warden," thought Charles. Holding the bolts up closer and angling them so the sunlight shone off their fletching, he suddenly inhaled sharply. "Holy Smokes, these are handmade, and I think I've seen this kind before. I wonder…" wonders Charles, a strange feeling of dread overtaking him. Giving himself a little shake, he quickly steps up the porch steps to join Amelia by the porch swing.

"Charles, why are you and Kay in such a hurry? You startled me, I haven't seen you this excited about anything since the sheep jumped the fences last spring," exclaims Amelia, surprised to see the usually stolid older man acting 20 years younger.

"I'm sorry, Amelia. I guess my mind was lost in thought. These bolts and the mystery out by the fence line have caused me to be in quite a stir," says Charles, as he smiles apologetically to Amelia, sensing she has more questions than he has time for now.

"Sorry, for the abrupt departure, dear, but I'll be in my room for a bit," says Charles.

“Ok, Charles, but Kay, you stay here with me girl,” says Amelia, patting the extra space next to her on the porch swing.

Charles hurried to his room and gets the fire safe from his closet. Taking the key hanging from around his neck, he opened the safe. “I know it’s in here somewhere,” whispers Charles to himself. He grabs the papers from the safe and tosses them onto the bed. Lying at the bottom of the safe was an envelope. On its face was written: Great Aunt Josephine. He took it to the window and removed its contents. The sun shone on a well-formed, but slightly charred, crossbow bolt which Josephine had given him along with the family journal. She told him when he was a child, that it was found by her father in the rubble after the fire of 1870, which burned the farmhouse to the ground.

This roused his suspicion about that drawing on the fence line even more. He remembered there were a few drawings in Aunt Josie’s journal. Searching through the pile of papers strewn over his bed, he finds her journal. Carefully flipping through the pages, one drawing stood out. A coat of arms with the black background and a red chevron across the center, but there were also three red lion heads. One each in the upper left and upper right of the shield and one center below the chevron.

“Oh, my Lord! This can’t be!” stutters Charles, stunned by the same symbols drawn within Aunt Josie’s journal. He sits on the edge of the bed staring at the drawing, thinking of his last, confusing conversation he had with his Aunt Josie before she went into the nursing home. His thoughts are drawn back nearly forty years, when Aunt Josie called him to her side. She was 95 years old and making her arrangements for when she passed, making sure her wishes were respected, which included passing on the family secrets to a young Charles.

“Now you will hold this story, this bit of family history, to your heart till your time comes or, heaven forbid, they return. If they were to return it is then, and only then, shall you reveal to our bloodline the task I have laid upon you. Always remember you are never alone, never without. Remember, when in need, our spirits will guide you,” says Aunt Josie.

“I must visit my old friend before I make a decision,” Charles says to himself, looking outward toward the northern part of the property where Grand Daddy sits. “We haven’t shared our thoughts in some time, but maybe Grand Daddy will set me on the proper path forward,” says Charles to himself, as he shuffles the papers back into an orderly arrangement to be able to put them back into the safe securely. He places the fire safe back into the closet but keeps the bolts and Aunt Josie’s journal with him, he quickly leaves his bedroom.

CHAPTER FOUR

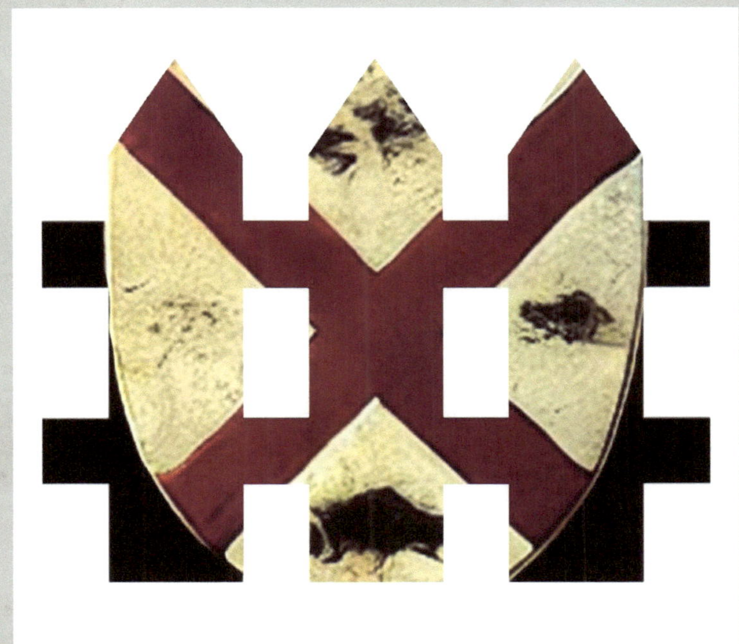

Ken entered the pasture and stopped to wait for his dad to close the south gate. When Gavin returned and buckled up, Ken drove as fast as he could while dodging boulders, and cow dung. He wanted to get the deer back and prepped for storage as soon as possible.

"What is that, Ken?" asks his father. Gavin was pointing to the quickly approaching north gate. Ken stopped and climbing off the Panther, walked up to the strange symbol drawn on the fence post.

"Never seen it before, Dad," says Ken. As Ken investigated the symbol, Gavin took a quick look around the area, but nothing else seemed out of the ordinary.

"I wonder if that's why your Grampa Charles wanted to talk to Griffin," says Gavin. Turning from the strange symbol, Ken had a thoughtful look on his face, "maybe," he says. "When did he say that, Dad," asks Ken, striding toward the Panther and climbing back on.

"When I called him to return the Panther, he said he needed to have a talk with Griff," Gavin replies, holding on to the back handles of the Panther as Ken starts the motor and slowly moves along the fence line looking for any other anomalous symbols.

"About what?" Ken asks.

"Something to do with the fence," says Gavin.

"That does look like something Griff might do. He's got heraldry drawings all over the walls in his room," says Ken, "he even has a few books covering all sorts of knights of the realm, or round table, in his room too."

"Yeah, I know. Too much time spent dreaming of valor and playing games on that tablet of his," says Gavin, grumbling to himself about how Griff is more interested in history and mythology than farming, but he is only twelve, Gavin remembers. Maybe he'll be a history teacher someday, Gavin thinks.

"He isn't too much into farming, is he Dad," says Ken, quietly.

"No, I think not," says Gavin, "he is too much a dreamer."

"Well, I think we better get that deer back to the shed and prepped," says Ken.

"Yep, let me open the gate and we'll be on our way," says Gavin. Gavin climbs off, pulls the chain and opens the gate, pulling it wide enough for them to drive through. Climbing back onto the Panther, he gestures forward "let's go."

Ken switches the Panther into a higher gear and speeds toward where he left the deer. The drive up the valley was uneventful, and Gavin was glad to see the herds of sheep, plus a few cows, were doing well. He'd have to check the water levels back at the farm's well monitors when he got back home. They followed an old path formed many years ago by their family who first settled here in the valley.

"Such a beautiful place, stop here for a second," asks Gavin. Ken slows the Panther and comes to a stop upon a bluff on the south edge of Lake Percival. The lake sits on the east side of Dee Run, the farms runoff stream, and then curves around southwest and eventually separates the Dafaid from for the Woodson farm.

"It's very peaceful here, Dad. I love coming up here," says Ken.

"Yes, I used to frequent Grand Daddy when I was young. The lake, trees, and especially the birds, the songs could always whisk you away to faraway lands full of adventure," says Gavin.

"Wow, Dad! I feel the same when I sit on Grand Daddy's throne seat," says Ken, energetically.

"Now, we better get your deer back to the farm," says Gavin.

"It's in the shade just a few feet behind Grand Daddy," says Ken. Pointing to the distant tree stump shaped like a throne, he slowed down as they approached the tall grass behind Grand Daddy, not wanting to hit the deer with the Panther's wheels.

"I don't see it!" says Ken, very confused because he knows where the deer was in relation to Grand Daddy.

"You in the right spot, Ken?" asks Gavin.

Ken jumps from the Panther and steps into the patch of grass where the deer had been. "This is the place, Dad. There's blood and you can see the blood trail from where I dragged it into the clearing," says an exasperated Ken as he walks around the area where the deer had been. He looks around for a trail or any indication of someone dragging the deer away.

"I don't see any sign of it being dragged off, and they even took the entrails. All we have left is a lot of blood," says Gavin. Ken drags his hand through his sandy colored hair and looks at his father, dumbfounded.

"What do you think, Dad? Would a bear do this?" Ken asks.

"I don't believe so, but if it did, then this place would be a mess and we'd have no trouble finding a trail," says Gavin, gesturing to the surrounding area that does not have the distinctive pattern a bear would leave behind. "Plus, I've never seen a bear up here. A few wolves and an odd coyote, but never bears," says Ken.

"Neither have I, but your Grampa Charles has, ask him when we get back home," says Gavin,

"I'll do that, Dad, but right now I've got a story of my own to finish. I need to find out who's been poaching on our farm," says Ken, pacing through the grass behind Grand Daddy and kicking the dirt in frustration. His father motions to the Panther, "We need to get back, Ken. I've got chores to finish, and you can help me."

"I'd like to stay here and look around a while longer, Dad. I won't be very long, and you can save those chores for me when I get back," says Ken, a beseeching look on his face as he faces his father.

"I don't think that's such a good idea. Someone was watching you when you gutted that buck. Heck son, they could be watching us right now!" says Gavin, trying to get through to his son the severity of the situation.

"Please, Dad! Whoever got the buck is long gone and I'm only going up Dee Run for a short distance, maybe I can find a blood trail," asks Ken.

"Sorry Ken, I can't let you do that alone. Let's get back and when the chores are done, I'll come back with you and we'll have a good look around, how's that sound?" asks Gavin, but without any indication that he expected a rebuttal. Ken, looking frustrated and slightly defeated, agrees.

"Yes Sir," says Ken, disappointed by the refusal, but understanding the need for caution, gets back on the Panther and waits to start the machine until Gavin has climbed on.

"We'll bring Kay with us. She's got the nose for scouting out a trail better than we do. We'll get to the bottom of this," says Gavin, setting his hand on his son's shoulder and giving it a comforting squeeze.

Ken lets out a slightly disgruntled laugh and pats his dad's hand on his shoulder. "Sure, Dad." He starts the engine on the Panther, and they wind their way back through the pastures, closing the north gate as they go.

CHAPTER FIVE

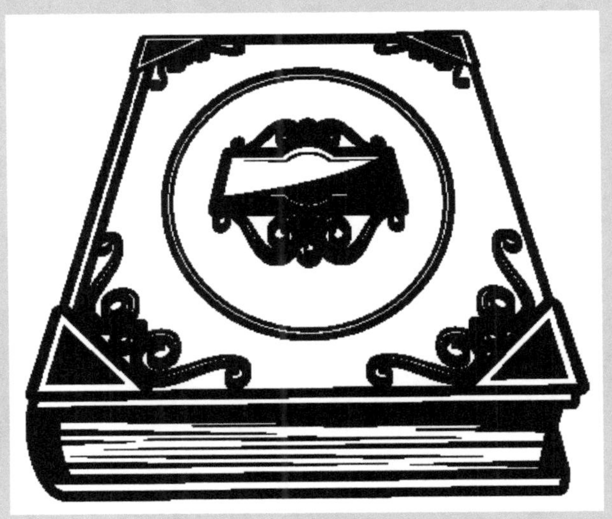

Charles stepped out onto the porch. Clutching the journal to his chest as he sat on the swing next to Amelia.

"What's that, Charles? Are you keeping a secret diary these days?" Amelia teased lightheartedly.

He pulled the journal away from his chest and gazed at it lovingly. He swiped his hand over the leather cover as if to remove any dust and gestured to Amelia with it. "No," he chuckled, "this is the 'Defaid Family' journal passed on to me by my Great Grandaunt Josephine back in 1980."

"Oh, how wonderful. Let's have a look," she says excitedly.

"I'm sorry, Amelia. I would love to tell you about the stories within these pages, but this isn't the right time. I must…" he pulled the journal close to his chest again protectively. He had to stop himself before he went too far and exposed secrets best left for the right person.

"You must what, Charles?" Amelia asks, worried at the sudden paleness of Charles's face. Rarely did see him so flustered and agitated, the normally stoic man was usually unflappable.

Kay, who was laying in front of Amelia, sat up and placed her front paw on Amelia's knee. She sensed the distress in her voice.

Charles reached over to Kay and patted her on the head, ruffling the border collie's head.

"It's okay, girl, not to worry. Just something on my mind," he says.

He turns toward Amelia and puts a comforting hand on her arm, "I'm fine, really. No need to worry. I'll explain another time," he says.

"Ok, Charles, I suppose so, but I'm gonna keep an eye on you just the same," says Amelia, still looking concerned and mildly worried. She places a hand onto his knee as she rose from the swing, "I'll be in the kitchen if you need anything."

"Has Gavin and Ken returned with that buck yet?" Charles asks.

"Not yet," says Amelia as she opens the screen door into the kitchen.

Charles gets up from the porch swing, letting it hit the back of his knees to stop its sway, and walked, with Kay by his side, over to the spot where to old house used

to stand. The only thing left from the 1870 fire were a few logs and what remained of a stone chimney. An open bare patch of dirt and grass separates the current house from the remnants of the old one, and picnic tables and a few chairs are scattered around a fire pit. Sometimes the family builds a fire and roasts hotdogs and marshmallows within it. Charles sits at the table and looks out toward the valley and the home of his old friend, Grand Daddy.

The snarl of the Panther's engine wakes Charles from his thoughts as Gavin and Ken come rumbling from behind the barn. They see him sitting at the picnic table and pulled up to him and turned off the engine.

"Where's that big buck at?" asks Charles, looking at the empty trailer and the frustrated faces of his son and grandson.

"It was gone when we got there," says Gavin.

"Grampa Charles, they took everything, guts and all!" complains Ken, loudly.

"Any sign, at all, of what did it?" asks Charles.

"No blood trail or sign of anyone disturbing the area," says Ken.

"If it was a bear or wolves, you'd think there'd be drag marks of some kind. Heck, the grass wasn't even bent over. It was like the buck just floated away," says Gavin, who waves his hands in the air as if the buck just floating away, was a normal occurrence.

Charles was silent for a few moments. His mind was still in a state on what to do in regard to Aunt Josie's journal and the drawings, and now this mystery with the missing buck, unease fills his chest and mind.

"Someone's been drawing on the fence out by the north gate, Dad. Is that why you wanted to talk to Griffin?" asks Gavin. He takes a seat at the picnic table next to his dad, and stares into the dead fire pit, rubbing this stubbled chin in thought.

"Yes, yes, it is. I forgot about that. Ken, would you go fetch him, I believe he's in the house," asks Charles.

"Ok, right after I put the Panther back in the shed," says Ken, but before he can take a step Charles motions for him to stay, "leave the Panther here Ken. I want to take a ride up to Grand Daddy in a bit," says Charles. Ken looks from his father to Grampa Charles and says, "Uh, Dad?"

“What’s wrong, Ken?” asks Charles.

“We don’t think it’s safe to be alone up there, right now, Dad,” says Gavin.

“I’m not gonna let some poachers scare me off my own land!” shouts Charles.

“Let me go with you, Grampa Charles. I just have a couple chores to finish, and we’ll be on our way. Is that ok with you, Dad?” asks Ken, turning toward his father eagerly. Gavin looked at Ken, a smile hovering around his lips, and laughing, he pats his son on his back, “Is that okay, with you Dad?” asks Gavin.

Charles looks between the two and thinks something happened up there by Grand Daddy between father and son, and the son just won. Smirking at the cleverness of the situation, Charles says, “Sure, I suppose, but we better take some food with us, the day is getting into afternoon, and we may not be back till late.”

Ken takes off toward the house with Kay close behind, leaving Grampa Charles and his father sitting at the picnic table, both silent as Ken enters the house.

A few minutes later, Griffin runs through the kitchen door. Seeing his grandfather and dad sitting at the picnic table, he heads that way. “What’s up? Ken said you wanted to talk to me,” the twelve-year-old, a bundle of energy, stands nervously in front of them, bouncing from foot to foot. He didn’t think he had done anything to earn the stern expressions on their faces, but it was only mid-day.

“Yes, I do. It’s about when I was checking the fence lines out by the north gate today. Did you draw anything on the north gates posts recently?” asks Charles.

“No, why?” asks Griffin, in confusion. He hadn’t been out to the north gate in a few days.

“I found a drawing of a shield on the gate this morning, black with a red chevron. I thought of you and your interest in the games and stories from the medieval times and wondered if you had drawn on the fence post,” asks Charles.

“No way, Grampa Charles!” exclaims Griffin.

“Your bedroom walls are covered with drawings of knights and swords. It is no big deal, Griff, but I was just curious, that’s all,” says Charles.

Griffin, with an alarmed look on his face, says “I wouldn’t do anything like that without permission, and even if I did it wouldn’t be that drawing,” says Griffin.

“Why, is there something different about it?” asks Gavin.

“It sounds very close to Morgana’s coat of arms,” says Griffin. He quickly runs back toward the house and slams the kitchen door shut in his haste. Charles and Gavin can hear Amelia’s shout not to slam the door, but in an afterthought way, because Griffin is in and out so quickly, it is a normal thing now.

“He probably went to grab one of his many mythology books, Dad,” says Gavin, to his father at the sudden departure of Griffin.

Just as quickly, and with another slam of the door and a remark from Amelia, Griffin runs up to the two men and opens a book on Arthurian legends to a page with coats of arms on it.

“See, Grampa Charles, that symbol you described is the coat of arms of Morgana,” says Griffin, displaying the open books description of the different medieval coats of arms.

“She’s a myth though,” says Gavin.

“I know, Dad, but if I were to draw on the gate it would be a red background with three gold shields or a red dragon, the one worn by Arthur and his knights,” argues Griffin, angry that he is being accused of vandalism. Of placing a symbol, he doesn’t even associate himself with, but an enemy of the knights he worships.

“Sorry, Griff, I didn’t mean to upset you,” says Grampa Charles, “we’re just trying to figure out where the symbols came from.”

“No problem, Grampa Charles,” says Griffin, smiling at his father and grandfather, “I guess I get a little too caught up on this stuff, it’s my favorite hobby. If you want to know more about knights and swords, or coats of arms, just ask,” he says.

“I’ll surely keep that in mind,” says Grampa Charles.

“I’ll have a look at it when I check the fence line tomorrow,” says Griffin.

“You’ll also find one on the northeast corner too,” says Charles.

“They put one there too?” asks Gavin.

“Who’s they Grampa?” asks Griffin, his interest in the mystery growing.

“We have no idea, Griff,” says Charles, looking forlorn.

"Let me take the Panther up there now, Dad. I've got to see this!" Griffin said excitedly as he headed toward the parked Panther.

"Ken and I are going up there in a few minutes, you can ride along if it's ok with your dad," says Charles, looking at Gavin. Gavin could see there was no stopping them when they were this set on exploring. His father and his youngest son were two peas in a pod. If there was adventure, then they would find or more exactly, it would find them.

"Can I, Dad," asks Griffin eagerly. Gavin could see the energy running through the body of is son, and no chores could compare to an adventure this summer day without letting him explore. Laughing, Gavin gave his father a quick disapproving glance, but said, "Ok, but no wandering off by yourself, understood?" he says sternly to Griffin, and by proxy, his father. They both grin at the excited yelp coming from the young boy.

"Yes! Dad, thanks," says Griffin, "I'll be right back, there's something that I want to bring along."

Gavin watched his son run up the stairs to the porch and grimaced as the door slammed closed, again. Hearing Amelia yell out again, he chuckled to himself, knowing that it was a lost cause right now.

"You'll have to keep a close watch on him. He tends to wander off sometimes. It's like once he has an idea, there's no turning him away from getting to the bottom of it," says Gavin.

"I remember a young boy who was just like him," laughs Charles. Gavin blushed, but nods, "True, not gonna lie, but I don't miss those days as much when I have the boys to watch," says Gavin.

"Yeah, I know what you mean," says Charles. They both sit back on the picnic chairs and reminisce about their younger days.

"He'll be fine though, Gavin," says Charles, reassuringly, "Ken and I will keep an eye on him.

Gavin sees the journal sitting on the picnic table, picking it up and running his hands over the old leather binding. "What's that your reading, Dad," asks Gavin.

Charles gestures for the book and Gavin hands it over. He watches his father gently run his hands over the leather, and wonders whose it was. "It's our family

journal. My Great Aunt Josephine entrusted it to me. It will be yours when I pass on. I better put this up before we leave," he says.

"I'd like to read it sometime soon. I never knew we had a family journal. Why bring it out now?" queries Gavin.

"Just something about those symbols on the gate, had me remembering Aunt Josie's stories, myths really, but I was interested in taking another look. I'll let you read it another time Gavin. Now, I should put this back before the kids and I head out," says Charles. Gavin watched as his father slowly walked back into the house, making sure not to slam the front door to the kitchen, and he continued to sit at the picnic table and enjoyed the view of the pastures. He loved this farm. A farmer was all he had ever wanted to be. His father was his guiding hand and always told him, "If you give to the land, the land will give back." Since he was a young man, whenever he thinks of that phrase, a strange feeling comes over him. He has no idea where it comes from, it's just there, and gives him strength of mind and body, like the will to persevere, to survive.

"Hey Dad, where's Grampa?" asked Griffin as he sits by his father on the picnic table. Gavin is surprised he didn't notice the door slamming, "must have been lost to my daydreams," he muses. Griffin laid a book on the table. "He went into the house for a minute. I'm surprised you didn't pass him," says Gavin.

"Ken told me about the deer. That's really weird," says Griffin.

"Yes, it is strange. What have you got there?" asks Gavin.

"It's a book on heraldry, you know, knights and stuff," says Griffin, pushing the book open and showing his father the coats of arms page, he was talking about earlier. "It gives a story about each one and who it belonged too and everything," says Griffin. "But I've pretty much figured out everything by now," says Griffin. He pulls the book toward himself and riffles through the pages, looking suddenly sad.

Gavin watches as Griffin picks at the splinters on the picnic table and tosses them into the grass. "You know, Griffin, it could be a new mystery for you to get into with your interest in English history, especially Arthurian legends," says Gavin, watching his son as he kicks his legs and swats at the bees buzzing around them. It was usually no problem for Gavin and Amelia to get Griffin excited about history, especially something he was interested in, but it was the start of the summer holidays and Griffin seems subdued, more interested in playing video games on his tablet with his friends than exploring.

Gavin picks up on the sudden change in his youngest son's mood, and trying to rouse his excitement once more, he asks, "You said it might be Morgana's coat of arms. How do you know that?" as Gavin.

Griffin pulled a folded paper from the pages of the book, opening it up he laid it out on the picnic table. It was large drawing showing the coats of arms arranged in a circular pattern, with several coats of arms at the bottom of the page. "I drew this for a class project last year. It's all the Knights of the Round Table and at the bottom are the most feared and hated enemies of the Round Table. That's how I remember Morgana's coat of arms," says Griffin.

"Oh, I remember you making this for school. This is very good, Griff! Where's Morgana's," asks Gavin, his interest peaked by his son's interest.

"It's the black and red one with the three lion heads," says Griffin, pointing to a page of the book that shows a picture of the coat of arms and gives a brief description.

"That's not exactly like the one on the gate, there's no lions," says Gavin, puzzled at the similarity, but not quite imagined it.

"I know, Dad, but it's got my interest," says Griffin.

"I suppose the ghostly looking guy in the upper right-hand corner is Merlin?" asks Gavin, pointing to the grayish outline of a man with long robes.

"Right, Dad. He's Arthur's mysterious wizard friend," says Griffin, smiling as he draws out mysterious, making it sound spooky.

Gavin chuckles along with Griffin, glad that his mood has picked up by talking about his favorite subject and having a mystery to solve. He remembers how long the summers were for him as a boy on the farm and having adventures throughout the summer days made them more bearable. He knows that the summer will be more chores and, boring, for the boy, and he is not happy about Ken leaving for college in the fall, but if having a mysterious adventure to keep him occupied all summer will keep him out of trouble, then it will be worth it.

"Best to put that away for now. Looks like you'll be heading out to the gate soon," says Gavin, pointing to the house as Ken and Charles head over in their direction.

"I see you've finished your chores," says Gavin. Ken looks down, but smiles ruefully, as he approaches his father and brother.

"Yes Sir, and I even swept out the shed," Ken says, giving Griffin a grim look.

"Oops, sorry Ken, I forgot," says Griffin. Ken quickly pulls his younger brother into a head lock, and they swat at each other, playfully.

"Come on, Ken, stop it," whines Griffin, as he wiggles about, trying to break his brother's hold on his head.

"Now, now boys, no time for that. Do you want to get going or not?" reprimands their Grampa. Ken lets go of his brother and dashes out of the way as the younger boy rounds on him and tries to get in a point of his own.

"I'm only teasing him, Grampa. Got to get it all out of my system this summer. Isn't that right, squirt?" asks Ken as the keeps just out of reach of Griffins hands and laughs at the vain attempts to wrestle him to the ground. Griffin, grumbles to himself and gives it one last chance to get one back at his brother, before admitting defeat. Gavin is glad to see that Griffin is smiling though, and sighs in relief.

"Those two will be the death of me before the summer ends," says Gavin to his father. They both watch the boys as they continue to push each other playfully, calling each other names as they all gather around the Panther.

"Time to go, boys," said Charles. He stood by the Panther's passenger side waiting for Griffin to enter first. "Gavin, would you let their mother know where we're headed. We should be back in an hour or two," says Charles.

"Will do, Dad," says Gavin.

"Then we're off," shouts Charles.

"Wait!" Gavin stands and waves his hands. "Dad, would you check the battery charge on the portable radio? I don't want you all to not have a way to contact us if there is an urgent need," says Gavin.

"I'll get it," says Ken, reaching into the dash and pulls out the handheld radio. "It still has power, about 3/4, and I've got my phone too," says Ken, reassuringly to his father.

"We've got it, Gavin. We know how well those things work in the valley. Just have

the radio near-by at all times or if worse comes to worse, we'll put out a smoke signal," Charles responds, laughing. Gavin sighs but smiles at the trio as they head out into the valley.

"I've got my phone too, Dad," yells Griffin, as the Panther gets further away. Their dog, Kay, sprints from the front porch and runs after the Panther, but Ken yells out, "Kay, stay!" The dog immediately stops, but whines at being left behind. Gavin calls her over to the picnic table where he is still sitting at, "You stay with me, girl. You might get hurt up there. We don't know who is poaching and wouldn't want you to get hurt."

CHAPTER SIX

Gavin looks at his watch, and says to Kay, "well, it looks like it's time for that cup of tea, girl. Let's go see what Amelia has been doing in the kitchen, smells pretty good." Smiling down at the dog, who sits quietly at his feet, her tail wagging, he heads for the house, making sure not to slam the front door. He enters the kitchen quietly, watching his wife as she sits at the kitchen table getting dinner ready, humming a tune to herself. She looks up and gives a quick smile when she sees who entered the kitchen.

"I was beginning to think you might still be out gathering up that deer with Ken," says Amelia. The kitchen smells like baking bread and chamomile tea and Amelia gets up from the kitchen table where she was chopping vegetables for the even meal and pours them a cup of the hot tea. A rainbow of colors shine through a prism hanging in the window. The kitchen has room for a large table adorned with a blue and yellow flowered tablecloth, and six chairs. An electric stove stands in the same spot that once housed the old wood stove and a shiny copper vent hangs where the stoves chimney once stood. New granite counter tops recently replaced the old white and gold sparkled Formica, and a large stainless-steel refrigerator sits near the stove.

"No, we've been back for some time," says Gavin, blowing on the hot tea, he takes a careful sip. The steam rolls up his face, giving this sun-soaked skin a nice facial.

"Is the deer ready for the freezer?" asks Amelia, as she continues chopping vegetables. Her knife making quick work of the routine preparations.

"The deer was gone when we got there," says Gavin, suspiciously. He reaches out and grabs a few stalks of celery before Amelia spots him.

"Really?" asks Amelia, tea pot in hand, she stills as she prepares to pour another cup for herself. "The poachers came back?"

"Yea, but it was weird," he says, taking a sip of how now, cooler tea.

"How so," asks Amelia. Taking the vegetables, she drops them into the pressure cooker, along with salt and pepper, before dropping in the prepared chicken breasts.

"I don't know how to explain it, Hun. There was a strange feeling by Grand Daddy, almost a protective aura around me and Ken, like it was guarding us from something," says Gavin, sipping his tea as he thinks about the feeling of warmth and safety he had felt near Grand Daddy earlier.

Amelia could hear the concern in Gavin's voice and see the worry etched into the lines on his face. She placed her hand on top of his that held his teacup, "I'd guess we all would be on guard if a poacher was in the area," she says, moving to the refrigerator she takes out the milk and butter, setting it on the counter.

"Yeah, I guess you're right, Hun. Must have been a poacher, but it was so weird that there was no trail of any kind," complains Gavin, watching as Amelia pours a measure of milk into the cooker and drops butter slowly around the dinner prep inside. She closes the lid and presses the timer, turning toward Gavin she smiles at him.

"Griff went by a bit ago, saying something about symbols and knights and how he wants to show something to Charles on his way out the door. What's that all about?" asks Amelia.

"Dad found a drawing on the north gate when he was checking the fence this morning and wanted to know if Griff had been drawing on the posts," says Gavin.

"Why does he think Griff had anything to do with that. It's not like him to go and do something like that," says Amelia, protective of her youngest child. Gavin smiles and, clearly trying to get Amelia to calm down says, "I know, Hun, but Dad just wanted to check all the boxes. You know how interested in legends about the Knights of the Round Table Griff is. It was in the shape of a shield. Similar to the ones hanging on Griff's walls in his bedroom. If he didn't have anything to do with it, then maybe he knows someone who did, or at least what they mean," says Gavin.

"Well, I can understand why Charles would immediately think of Griffin, but I'm sure he didn't have anything to do with it," says Amelia, setting her teacup down with irritation.

"No, we talked to Griff, and he says he didn't do it and even went and got a book of Arthurian legends that had coats of arms in it to show us. The one on the fence wasn't exactly like the one in the book and Griff was upset about that," says Gavin.

"Oh, really," says Amelia.

"Yep, he was a bit upset with his Grampa for thinking he would do such a thing, especially when the drawing resembled someone named Morgana's coat of arms," says Gavin. He laughed at the memory of a frustrated Griffin showing the symbol from the book.

“Well, if anybody would know, it would be Griffin, he’s a whiz at that stuff,” says Amelia.

“That he is,” says Gavin.

“Maybe one of the Woodson boys did it. There always up to no good,” says Amelia.

“Most likely,” says Gavin.

“Is Griff with Charles?” asks Amelia.

“Yeah, he went with Dad and Ken up to look at the drawing out by the north gate and then on up to Grand Daddy. Dad wanted to visit with Grand Daddy while Ken and Griff hunt for any clues to who took the deer. Probably, to see if there is any sign of where the thieves might have gone to. Those lowlands have many streams and trails running to the lake and back into the trees,” says Gavin.

“Really Gavin! The poachers could still be up there,” says Amelia, alarmed.

“Hun, it’s okay. I’m sure the poachers are long gone; they got what they came for. The boys will be fine. Dad will keep a close eye on them,” says Gavin. Amelia does not look so sure. She knows how much those boys love to explore, and Charles is only interested in sitting with Grand Daddy.

“I’m not so sure who should be keeping an eye on whom. Charles was acting a bit strange today when he joined me on the porch this morning. He had a little leather book with him and said it was a journal from some Great Aunt of his, Josie I believe,” says Amelia.

“Yeah, he had it on the picnic table when we returned,” says Gavin.

“Did he let you look through it?” asks Amelia.

“No, he said I would eventually get to look through it ‘one of these days’,” says Gavin, making finger quotes with his fingers. Amelia smirked; she could tell he was irritated.

“I asked as well. He’s being secretive about this journal,” says Amelia.

“I think these drawings have spooked him some. He’ll come around when he feels ready,” says Gavin. “I have a feeling he may know more that he is letting on, but he seems almost scared. We’ll have to wait and see.”

“Well, it is unusual for him to be so mysterious, but it’s hard to tell what is running through is head when he doesn’t want to share something. He was worked up about that drawing on the north gate,” says Amelia. Sighing, she starts to clean up the kitchen. Gavin stands and gives her a hug, “thank you for being here. I don’t know what I would do without you.” She turns around in his arms and wrapping her arms around his neck, gives him a peck on the lips.

“Gavin, it will be alright. I know your worried, with Ken leaving soon, Griffin, well, being Griffin, and your dad slowing down, but I have faith in this family, in you,” Amelia gives him a quick hug back and puts her head on his shoulder. They sway back and forth, listening to the late afternoon sounds.

CHAPTER SEVEN

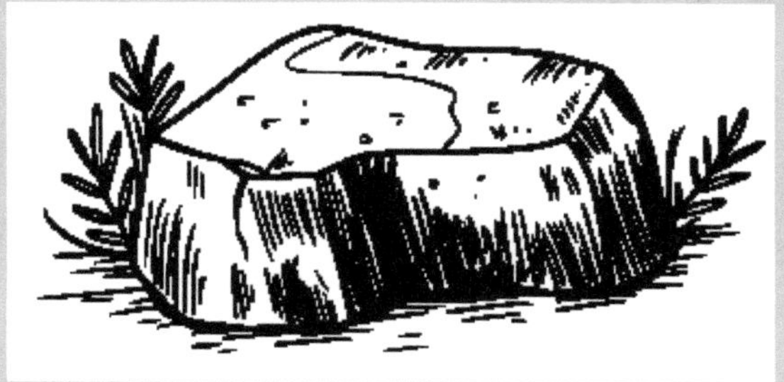

Andras took a brief minute to check his pouch and quiver for the second time. No longer is he that young, tall, and raven-haired squire. His strength matched only by his faith. Now his strength has faded, forgetful at times, with a slight limp from on old leg wound, and more than a few gray hairs, but his faith endures. Time has never been able to drag that down, it grows stronger with each day. Loyalty to his God and countrymen will never wane.

"Grigor, have you everything you'll need?" asked Andras. He could tell something was upsetting the lad.

"I've lost my brush, Andras!" Grigor cried franticly.

"Good heavens boy, you're acting like a squire who's lost his knights shield," exclaimed Andras, watching an anxious Grigor search through the bags for his missing brush.

"But I just had it, Andras! It has to be here somewhere," says Grigor.

"We have no time for this foolishness, Grigor. We Fall in a few minutes. There's no time to make another, you'll have to use your quill," says and exasperated Andras.

"Right, but it will look like…well, it'll look terrible," says Grigor.

"Do you have everything else accounted for, then lad?" asks Andras.

"I do, Andras. Here's my quill, my crossbow, quiver, and my pigments," says Grigor.

"How many bolts do you have?" asks Andras.

"Ten, I think," says Grigor, setting down his pack and checking his quiver for the number of bolts he should have. "Yes, ten it is," says Gregor, putting this pack and quiver on his back for the journey.

"What is that on the ground, there by your boot, then?" asks Andras.

"My brush! It must have dropped from my quiver, but how?" asks Grigor quietly to himself as he bends down and picks up the brush. He dusts the dirt off of it and slots it over this shoulder and into the quiver.

"Never mind that for now. We must be on our way," says Andras. He is relieved that everything with the young man is in order for their journey. "Gather your gear and let's head for the stone."

The two men follow a well-worn path through the woods, taking in the quiet silence surrounding them as they walk through the trees. Sunlight slants through the branches, creating an enchanted aura as they walk.

“Listen Grigor, I know this is your first Fall, and I know you are nervous, but that is understandable. When you see the mist forming around us, remain calm. Just step into it as if you are entering a doorway. Remember what you’ve been taught, and you will uphold yourself well,” says Andras.

“I will, thank you,” says a nervous Grigor. He had faith in what the Elders had taught him. Of the many things they passed on to him were these words that were foremost in his mind right now, ‘Fear not thine enemy.’

“We’ll only be there long enough to leave the warnings, and whatever you do, don’t get lost in what you see or hear. This is a totally different world from ours,” warns Andras.

“I remember the Elders were very emphatic about that Andras, when they talked to me about this task. A question, though Andras, that has been bothering me. The Elders, when they spoke to me, their speech was clear to me, but when I saw them conversing amongst themselves, I heard not a word, nor did their lips move. How is that possible, Andras?” asks Grigor.

“There are those among us that have higher powers, such as the Elders,” says Andras, quietly.

“Our Seeker must have great powers to see the mission we are about to Fall for, mustn’t he Andras? The Elders never say how our Seeker knows such things,” says Grigor.

“It is through the Elders themselves that our Seeker knows of these things, and not for men such as us to try to figure out,” says Andras.

“There is much that I do not understand,” mumbles Grigor.

“Never fear Grigor, you will learn more as you progress with your training,” says Andras.

Both were silent for the remainder of their trek. The Stone lay deep within a box canyon whose walls rose sharply on either side of a stream, which found its way through the winding corridor. Many times, their feet were refreshed and cleansed when crossing its cool waters. Finally, they reached their destination. The walls opened and allowed the daylight to expose a mound centered in the opening surrounded by ferns and wildflowers. On top of the mound lay a large flat stone, circular in shape. Water fell, almost silently, as if the glade was enchanted and nary a sound could be carried through the grasses and flowers. Steppingstones were placed across the stream for access to the mound.

"Oh, Andras, the Lord has truly put his hand into making this wondrous sight," gasped Gregor, as he took in the surrounding area. "The air and stones are calling to me in ways I have never felt before."

"It is how the Elders know, Grigor," says Andras.

"How they know?" asked Grigor.

"This is the place that the Elders come when they feel their kindred calling out for aide," says Andras.

"Which Elder are we doing this Fall for, Andras?" asks Grigor.

"Only our Seeker knows who this Fall is for," says Andras.

"Why shouldn't we know, we are the ones…" asks Grigor.

"No time for questions, now. We must prepare for our journey," says Andras. He slowly walks up the mound until he is standing in front of the large stone. He motions for Grigor to step upon the stone. "This, Grigor, is the 'Stone of Return.' You must first be seen by the spirits in order for your abilities to manifest and be ready for the journey ahead," says Andras.

"Why was I not talked beforehand about this acceptance?" asked Grigor, as he stood by the edge of the stone. Hesitancy kept him from continuing onward; he had not been informed of any such task before he could continue the journey.

"The only way forward for a trainee is to go through this process and be fully accepted, received, and seen by the spirits. You were not told, because of the necessity for purity, courage, and faith," says Andras.

"What must I do then, Andras? How will I know if I am to be accepted?" asks Grigor.

"The Stone will show you," says Andras.

Grigor, not happy with the cryptic answers he is being given, has faith that everything will be as it should be as he steps up onto the stone. As he sets foot into

the exact center of the stone, and he turns to look at Andras, an overwhelming feeling takes over his body. “Andras, I cannot move!” shouts Grigor.

“Patience my boy, and have faith,’ offers Andras.

A strange sensation overcomes his mind, it seems like his body is floating in the air, but looking down at his body, he is still standing on the stone. Then a disembodied voice shouts out into the glade, ‘Never Without!’ After that the sensation of floating dissipates and he finds himself back within his own mind and body, standing on the stone. The next thing he is aware of is Andras standing by his side.

“Welcome back, brother!” cries Andras, clasping the younger man by the shoulders.

“What happened? It felt like I was floating, but I wasn’t…” asks a perplexed Grigor.

“You were accepted by the ’Stone of Return,’ and given the honor of becoming my brother in full. Now, you will find answers to all your questions soon, Grigor. Now, face the water and see how it flows down the wall. The mist will rise from it and, as it comes near, we shall enter,” says Andras.

Grigor, overjoyed to be a considered a brother, and accepted within the company of such men as Andras, he turns to face the wall of water as it flows gently down from above. As the water flows by their feet, a mist begins to form, making the glade seem to disappear within its formless grasp. They stepped forward into the mist and were immediately engulfed in white and seemed to vanish into the very air.

As his foot hit the ground, Grigor knew they were in another world. There was a warm breeze, and the sun flickered through the trees, dappling the leaves of the trees in brilliant greens of every type. Birds could be heard in the forest surrounding them, and a large stone set in the middle of a clearing stood as their entry point into this new world. A small stream gently ambled past, creating a pleasant resonance that accompanied the bird song.

Grigor looked around in confusion, “What! That quick! I thought it would take more effort to get through the mist,” says Grigor, looking at Andras for answers.

“That’s why it’s called a Fall, Grigor,” chuckled Andras. “Now let us be off. There’s a fence that needs our attention.”

Grigor stepped from the stone and followed Andras as he made his way toward a

small track through the trees. "If this world has a stone. Do all the worlds that we enter have a stone as well?" asks Grigor.

"Most do, but not all," says Andras.

"Why not all worlds, Andras?" asks Grigor.

"Some were lost in battle many years ago, while others our enemies discovered and destroyed trying to prevent our entry into those worlds," says Andras.

"Then the enemy does not know that we can make a Fall without the use of the Stones?" asks Grigor.

"Oh, they do know my brother, but not how that is undertaken. Since they have learned about our ability to travel without the aid of a Stone, no Stone has been harmed, but our secrets are still safe from their hands, and must remain so," warns Andras.

They follow a stream for some time till they come to a lake. The small track they were following letting out as they entered the surrounding lake lands. They knelt on the lake shore and surveyed their surroundings.

"This is a bit different than when I was last here," says Andras.

"You've been here before, Andras?" asks Grigor.

"Many years ago, our enemies, the Evil Ones, tried to destroy this farm," says Andras.

"What happened," asked Grigor.

"By the time we got the bloodline "accepted," the house had been set on fire and was burnt to the ground. But the one who was "accepted" was able to drive the enemy from his and," says Andras.

"Is the "accepted" one still here?" asked Grigor.

"No, he has passed on, but his descendants still live here, and the Elders say that they have a strong bloodline connected to the spirits. We must find and do what we can to keep them from harm till they are "accepted," says Andras.

"What is that smell, Andras," says Grigor, grimacing at the foul odor that permeated the area they knelt in.

Andras raised up and sniffed the air, and quickly returned to his knee, "stay low,

Grigor! Our enemy is near," warned Andras. He sniffed the air again and looked around, keeping low in the scrubby grass next to the lake shore. "They must have been to our west across the lake. Their odor is fading quickly. I believe we can move on from here, but be vigilant," warns Andras.

Andras and Grigor walked through the thickening trees and grasses that surrounded the lake. Bird song accompanied them as they traversed the lake. The trees evened out as they approached a wide field of grasses.

"I see that gate to the farm," says Grigor.

"Yes, I do as well, Grigor. Now we must be careful not to be seen by the farmer. The north gate is the most likely place for a marker to have been placed by our enemy.

"Why there, Andras," asked Grigor.

"The farther out the markers, the less likely for them to be seen and interrupted. The markings left are an evil portent to the bloodline," says Andras. Grigor gets out his painting materials and places over top the black shield with its red chevron a red dragon symbol.

"By doing this step, we are openly redeclaring our protection of the bloodline who lives here. We will be ever vigilant against the designs of the enemy," says Andras. He looks at the painting done by young Grigor and with a hearty clap on his back, Andras congratulates Grigor on a job well done. "You handle the brush very well, Grigor. I will let the Elders know. They have been wanting the old shields touched up," says Andras. He suddenly pulls himself and Grigor back into the shade of the trees, "listen!"

"What is that noise?" asks Grigor, who is trying to see into the north field, but Andras is pushing him back into the tree line.

"A machine! Gather the gear, we must leave now!" says Andras, who urgently gestures to Grigor to stash away his paints and brushes. Hastily, the two men push into the trees and crouch down into the scrubby grass. Making their way back around the lake, they find the path toward this worlds Stone of Return. Andras looks behind them and motions for Grigor to halt and they hunch down into the gathering shade of the trees "We must stop here, Grigor. We cannot keep this pace if we wish to remain unseen. We will lay low until it is clear, and then move," urges Andras. In the distance, through the trees, Andras sees a strange machine stop and 3 people disembark from it, two boys and an older man.

CHAPTER EIGHT

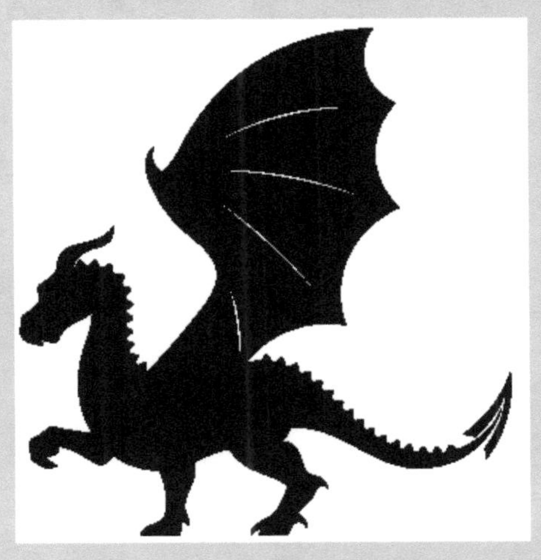

"Ken, you might want to slow down a bit," warns Charles.

"Sorry, Grampa!" says Ken, as he quickly brings the Panther to a steady stop.

"Yeah, I think we hit every rock in the pasture," whines Griffin, rubbing his backside ruffly.

"The only rock in this nature is the one on your shoulders," chuckles Ken, who quickly steps out of the way of his brother's shove.

"Oh, you're so funny, ha-ha!" calls out Griffin, pouting.

"Okay, you two, let's try to get along, we have important things to do," says Charles.

"Sorry, Grampa," says Ken and Griffin in unison.

They hadn't walked close enough to open the north gate yet when Ken came to a sudden stop. "Grampa can you see the drawing on the gate? It's changed since I last saw it this morning," says Ken. He walks up to the gate and stares in confusion at the sudden appearance of a different symbol.

"All I can see is a red splotch from over here, give me a minute," says Charles as he walks closer to the gate, squinting at a slowly crystallizing symbol of a red dragon.

"What the heck is going on here?" shouts Charles when he sees the symbol on the gate. Griffin takes a step closer and peers inquisitively at the red dragon symbol.

"Where's the black shield? All I see is a red dragon, but I can see something behind it," says Griffin.

"It has been covered by this red dragon design, but that makes no sense, not that this makes any darn sense to me," groused Charles. Charles stomps closer to the gate and stares furiously at the strange new symbol. Griffin reached up and touched the red color with his index finger, and a wave of dizziness overtakes him. Ken grabs onto his arm to keep him from falling to the ground.

"What happened Griff, are you Okay?" asks Ken, searching his brothers face for any indication of illness.

Griffin regained his balance. "I think so. When I touched the dragon, I got really dizzy. I. I'm okay now," he says.

"I think we better go home, boys," says Charles.

"No, Grampa, please! I'm good, really. Just hungry. I didn't eat any breakfast this morning. I brought this granola bar, see. I'll be fine after I eat this," says Griffin, trying for reassuring, but not being very convincing since he was a little pale.

"I've seen him do this before, Grampa. He'll be okay once he has had something to eat, really," says Ken.

As Griffin finished of the granola bar, color did return to his cheeks. He opened the book on heraldry, flipping straight to the page with the necessary information on the red dragon symbol. "This dragon is almost identical to the dragon on the flag of Whales," says Griffin. He held the book up next to the image on the gate.

"Wow, you're right Griff! What do you think Grampa?" asked Ken.

Charles tried to keep calm and not let go his emotions. "Well, I'm not sure, but I do believe someone is playing games, of which, I do not like," says Charles.

"We should check out Grand Daddy, Grampa," says Griffin, suddenly worried for the old tree stump.

"Good idea, Griff. Open the gate so I can pull the Panther through," says Ken.

"I'm not too sure about this Kenrich. Something does not feel right," says Charles, who looks worried and a bit frazzled. Ken is suddenly not as enthused about this adventure now. If Grampa Charles is worried, then they should be careful as well.

"It's alright Grampa Charles," says Griffin with enthusiasm despite the sudden charge in the air. Ken and Charles look at one another, concerned, but willing to push through to Grand Daddy, at least. Griffin's senses were on high alert ever since he touched that dragon image on the gate. He didn't understand how, but he knew they were free of any danger.

Charles gazed with admiration upon his young grandson. He could see Griffin displayed the same traits as his Great Grandaunt Josephine and his confidence was infectious.

"Then lead the way young man," says Charles, gesturing for Griffin to take the lead.

Griffin opened the gate and waited for Ken to clear the entrance with the four-wheeler and then closed and secured it before returning to the Panther.

"It's been a while since I was last up to visit Grand Daddy. I hope he's not weathered too much," says Charles.

“He looked to be in good shape when I was up here earlier, Grampa,” says Ken, reassuringly. They took the westward path around Lake Percival and stopped at Grand Daddy.

“What is that smell!” says Griffin, holding his nose over the pungent aroma that seemed to be everywhere. His senses were on high alert, danger was near.

“Smell? I don’t smell anything,” says Ken.

“Might be the blood, over there, from that deer?” says Charles, pointing out the smashed grass that was covered in the blood of the animal. He also caught an unfamiliar odor but kept it to himself.

“I did smell something, but it must have been passing by in the wind,” says Ken.

Griffin relaxed and climbed off the Panther. He walked around the clearing and turned toward Ken, “Yeah, the smell is gone now, weird. Where’s the blood trail Ken?” asks Griffin. He felt a strong urge to find out where the trail of blood would take them. Ken was standing several feet from where he had field stripped the deer. “Over here, Griff. It’s headed north, follow me!” says Ken.

“Be alert, boys,” says Charles, “this has been a strange day, so stay together.”

Ken and Griff followed the blood trail to Dee Run. “This is where it ends, Griff,” says Ken. The small stream meandered past them, carrying any further trail along with it.

“Did you check on the east side of the stream, Ken?” asked Griffin.

“Yeah, for about a hundred yards, but I wanted to get that buck back to the shed before the sun could spoil it,” shouts Ken, as he walks up the side of the stream, looking for footprints, or anything to explain how that deer disappeared.

“Where did you find the other bolt?” asked Griffin.

Ken turned and pointed at a nearby oak tree. “If it wasn’t for that Cardinal I wouldn’t have found it. Heck, there might be others out there,” says Ken. He turns quickly scanning the trees, looking for any further feathered bolts.

“Could you tell from what direction it came from?” asked Griffin, as he walked up through the scrubby lake grass towards the tree the bolt had been stuck in. Upon looking further, he could see how deeply indented the bolt must have been. “They must have been close by,” thought Griffin to himself.

“From the north,” Ken said, pointing toward the northern most part of their property, which was mainly rocky fields and hills.

“Did you give them to Grampa Charles?” Griffin asked, eager to see the bolts for himself.

“Yeah, Griffin, I’d never seen that kind before and I thought, maybe, Grampa would know more about them,” says Ken.

“Maybe that buck was here getting a drink when it was shot. The first shot could have missed and that’s the one you found in the tree,” speculated Griffin, who had a strange urge to continue further north. “Let’s follow Dee Run north, Ken. You didn’t check west of it, maybe we’ll get lucky,” says Griffin, excited at the chance to be on an adventure.

“Hey, little brother, you need to spend more time in the woods. You’re pretty good at this outdoorsy stuff,” joked Ken.

Griffin laughed, “Thanks Ken, but I think I’ll leave the hunting to you, and Kay.”

They put a short distance between them and walked north for some time, looking for anything that would help them find the poacher, or more indications of where the deer may have gone. “Find anything, Griff?” yelled out Ken. He got no response and looked to the right for his brother. “Darn it, Griff. You’re always wandering off! Why’d I think you’d be good in the woods?” grumbles Ken. Ken returned to Grampa, who was sitting on Grand Daddy, “Have you seen Griff?” They checked the surrounding woods, but saw no trace of the young boy, “Griffin!” they called out.

CHAPTER NINE

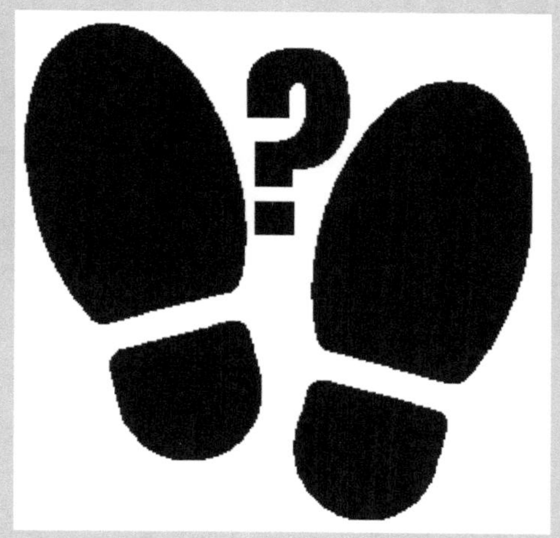

Andras could hear the sputtering sound of the side-by-side as it passed within a few feet of a fallen tree limb that was providing their cover.

"I feel a strong presence coming from them, Andras," said Grigor.

"Yes, as do I. We may have located the one the Elders told me of. Let us see what they are up to. They're heading to the western shoreline. We'll keep a good distance east of the lake and see what they do. Let's go," says Andras.

They moved north at a slow pace and just far enough from the lake to stay out of site. On occasion, Andras and Grigor would stop and get close enough to peer over the lake when they knew they could no longer hear the engine noise.

"What are they doing?" asked Grigor.

"They've left that strange contraption they were riding on and walked behind a large stump. I cannot see them now. Hold on, there's one stepping into the stump and sitting down. The other two are walking into the trees. The one sitting on the stump is the older one, with grey hair and the other two are the young boys. The taller one looks to be the older of the two," says Andras.

"Shouldn't we keep moving?" asked Grigor, getting nervous.

"Not yet, Grigor. The two young ones are now walking north. They're looking at a trail or something on the ground and the taller one is pointing in a northeasterly direction. As it stands now, our paths could cross. We'll stay back a bit and see where it is they're off too," says Andras.

The two boys stopped when they came to the stream. "They've halted at the stream," says Grigor. He could see that something had caught the boy's attention on the eastern side of the stream toward the glade the Stone of Return was located.

Grigor whispered, "they'll find the stone!"

Andras did not look worried and tried to calm down his young companion, "it will be okay. They can do nothing to the stone, and we have time on our side."

"They keep moving, heading further north, and staying on the western side of the stream. They seem to be looking for something specific, Andras," says Grigor.

"We'll give them a bit and then I want to inspect that spot that they just left. I think I might know what they are looking for. Grigor, I want you to keep pace with them, but I will not be far behind. If you reach the stone alone, stay hidden till I arrive," says Andras.

Grigor gave an affirmative not, and silently moved onward. Andras watched the two boys as they went deeper into the trees and then out of site. Andras checked to see if he could be seen by the older man sitting by the lake and was relieved that the trees blocked further inspection from that direction. Cautiously approaching the narrow stream, he stepped across using a large stone, to keep his feet dry. Immediately, he scanned the ground as he dropped to a knee. "Yes, I was right! It was a blood trail they were following."

Grigor followed the boys till they went out of site, just east of the stone, waiting there till Andras arrived. Several minutes went by when he heard a groan. Looking in the direction of the stone, he was stunned to see the younger boy climb up onto the stone. He was just barely tall enough to make the climb. He was grunting and groaning till he gained a good grip and pulled himself up. Grigor stared in disbelief when the boy stepped into the center of the stone and turned to grin at the older lad, before suddenly disappearing in a cloud of mist.

"Griffin!" yelled Ken, racing toward the stone.

Grigor couldn't believe what was happening. He watched as the older boy climbed the stone and moved from edge to edge searching for his brother without success. The trees parted and he turned happy to see Andras, "Somethings happened, Andras," whisper shouted Grigor. Andras looked toward the stone and could see the older boy standing on top of it, "Grigor, are you okay?"

"The young one! He was on the stone, and, and now he is gone. The mist swallowed him up," says Grigor, who urgently pointed at the stone, where the other lad had sat down in confusion.

"Gone! You mean he fell through the mist?" asks an unbelieving Andras.

"Yes!" says Grigor.

"We must Fall back into our own world, Grigor. The dangers he could face are many," says Andras urgently. They turned toward the stone and watched the older boy give the stone and the glade another once over and climb down from the stone. They watched as he ran past their hiding spot calling for the older man. The two looked at each other and quietly, but quickly, moved toward the stone and mounted it in preparation for their departure from this world. Both were worried what fate could have befallen the young lad, even though it has only been minutes since he transitioned into the mist.

"Will he be there, Andras, when we Fall through?" asked Grigor.

"We can only hope," says Andras, trying to sound confident, but even he was not sure what would happen to the boy. They stepped into the mist and appeared on their worlds Stone of Return.

Grigor looked quickly around, "He's not here, Andras. Where could he have gone?"

Andras turned and relief flowed through him. He motioned for Grigor to turn around with him and he saw a familiar face approaching from the trees, with the boy by his side.

"Master Seeker, it is good to see you," says Andras.

"Men, I want you to welcome our most recent, and I might add, our youngest ever 'accepted,'" says the Seeker.

"How did you know he had Fallen?" asked Grigor.

"The Elders sensed there was a strong spirit near your Fall location. Therefore, I've kept a watchful eye since your departure. I knew we would have a visitor, but I wasn't expecting one with such strength of mind and heart," says the Seeker.

"Then he knows?" asked Andras.

"Aye, that he does, and so much more. May I introduce you to Griffin Defaid, Seeker," says the older Seeker. Both men were speechless as they stood with widened eyes gazing upon the young Seeker.

"Griffin, since these two have lost their tongue, I will speak for them. This is Squire Andras, soon to be Knight Andras. That is if he can get his voice back," said the older Seeker, smiling. Andras regained his composure and reached for Griffin's hand, "Sorry, Seeker Griffin! Welcome."

"And this is Squire Grigor. I believe you both have this day in common. Am I correct Squire Grigor?" gently asking the still speechless Squire.

"Aye, Master Seeker. Welcome Seeker Griffin. It seems that we are now brethren as we both were 'accepted' on the same day," says Grigor, smiling down at the young boy.

Griffin stood motionless, trying to take in his surroundings. "Hello, I think," he says with trepidation, and considerable confusion. His mind was still trying to keep up with what the Master Seeker has awakened within him. He was amazed at what he was looking at, a Knight and his Squire, and a magician, at least they seemed to be to him. The Master Seeker had dark flowing robes, the color of the forest green surrounding them, and if that didn't scream, magician, he didn't know what to say.

"Andras, he must be returned to his own world. He will be missed," says the older Seeker.

"Aye, Master Seeker. We shall return him, but does he know about his strengths?" asks Andras.

"I have awakened his abilities, and now he must quickly learn to control them," says the older Seeker.

"Come, Seeker Griffin. Grigor and I shall accompany you back to your own world," says Andras. Griffin steps toward the two men, "Fare-the-well my young Seeker," says the older Seeker, waving to the trio as they fade into the mist.

As the mist cleared on the other side of the world's divide, Andras made certain that Griffin was on steady feet. Griffin turned and faced his escorts. "I'm scared! The Master Seeker said I would learn to use the strengths given to me in my own time. What am I to do? Will you help me?" asks Griffin, fighting back tears. Andras faced the young boy and smiling, placed a reassuring hand onto his shoulder. "Young Seeker, we may not remain behind to aid you, but be assured that the Master Seeker would not have left you without aide," says Andras. He gestures around them, taking in the stream and trees of the glade, and surrounding forest. "Now is your time, Seeker Griffin. This forest is your home. You must protect what is yours and hone the strengths that have been awakened. The abilities will come intuitively to you with time," says Andras. "Remember, you are never without. We will always be by your side."

"Farewell Seeker Griffin, Byth Heb!" says Grigor. Waving, the two men stepped to the Stone and were swallowed by the mist once again. Griffin stood on the stone for some time, trying to control his conflicted emotions about what just happened. He wondered, for a minute, if this was real or just a wild daydream of his from reading too much about knights and sorcery on his tablet.

"Griff, Griffin!" yelled out Ken. He could see him running through the trees towards where he was standing. Quickly, he jumped down from the stone and tried to play as nonchalantly as a 12-year-old could. "What's all the yelling?"

"Where have you been? I've been looking all over the place for you. You don't just disappear like that," shouted a relieved Ken, hugging Griffin close to him. Griffin took a second to appreciate being back with his family, but then pushed Ken away and said playfully, "I've been right here."

Ken, relieved to see Griffin was okay, calmed himself down and asked, "Then why didn't you answer me when I called your name?"

Griffin was not ready to explain what had just happened to him, he wasn't sure if he even knew how to explain it. Quickly, he comes up with a story about seeing another Cardinal in the trees and racing off to see if it would lead him to another bolt or signs of where the deer might be. Ken looked disapprovingly at him, "I was so worried. You know that there were poachers in the area recently, you could have been hurt," scolded Ken.

"I know, my mind was in another place, Ken. I'm sorry," says Griffin, relieved that he was able to invent a story that was believable. He hated to lie to his brother, but he saw no other option at that moment.

"Never let that happen again, Griff! Promise," says Ken.

"I promise," says Griffin, smiling weakly to hide his regret. He knew that promise could never be fulfilled.

"We need to get back to Grampa," says Ken, heading out of the glade toward the path into the trees. "I take it you found no sign of the poachers or blood trails?"

"No, there was nothing besides the normal animal trails, and no other bolts either," says Griffin.

Staying to the west of the Dee Run, the boys began their return to Grand Daddy, and their Grampa.

"Did you know that big stone was up there, Ken?" asks Griffin, curiously.

"Yeah, I call it the Bathing Stone," says Ken.

"What? You take baths on it," cried Griffin, laughing at the image.

Ken thought for a few seconds and laughed, "Yeah, I guess you could say that, but not with soap and water."

"Oh, I gotcha, you sunbathe on it. That's cool, Ken!" says Griffin.

"Right Griff, now you're catching on," says Ken.

"I don't get up there often. Maybe a couple times in the summer, and once in the fall to check for deer sign," says Ken.

"Like rubbing and tracks?" asks Griffin.

"Yeah," says Ken.

Griffin thought hard about his next question. He didn't want to make his brother nervous or suspicious about why he was so interested in the stone. "How does being up here make you feel? You know, relaxed or happy?" inquired Griffin.

"I get a nice warm feeling when I'm up here, I suppose. It makes me feel good when I lay out on my towel and when I get to my feet this amazing feeling of rightness, comes over me. It doesn't make sense, but I feel like I have to defend the whole area, but that's probably from the adrenaline of jumping off the stone," says Ken. Griffin stops suddenly, looking around, he smells a nasty odor. "There's that rotten smell again, Ken. Can you smell it?" asks Griffin.

"Yeah, man that really stinks!" says Ken. He turns and checks the direction of the wind the smell is strongest and yells, "That's by Lake Percival. Grampa Charles, come on Griffin!" shouts Ken. Both boys run down the side of the stream, the pathway clear of debris as they hurry toward their grandfather, and possibly into danger.

CHAPTER TEN

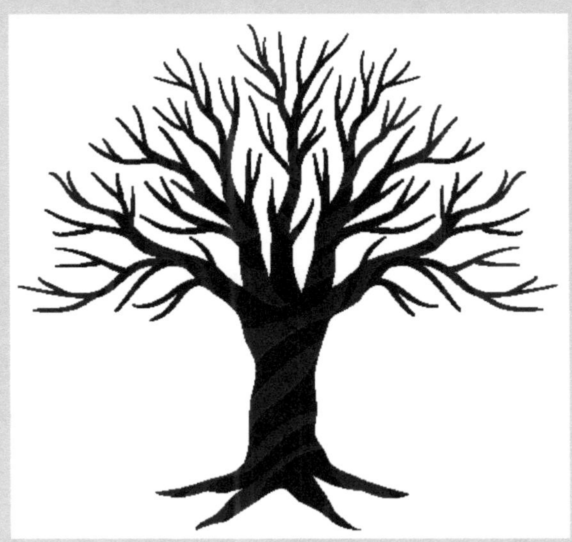

Charles entered Grand Daddy and watched his two grandsons disappear into the forest. Taking a seat within the tree stump, and giving the tree stump a loving pat, he turned toward Lake Percival. "I'm sorry, old friend, for not visiting as often as I should. Please forgive me. I wish this was a time for us to relax and share a smile, but I'm afraid there is trouble coming. I hope you can help me decide the proper course to take."

He sat in silence, enjoying the sounds of the lake and the leaves rustling in the breeze. A calmness came over him and he drifted off to sleep. Sometime later, he was awakened by the same foul smell they had experienced earlier. This time, though, it was accompanied by a loud, gruff, voice coming from behind him. He slowly raised himself up to peer over the back of Grand Daddy,

Standing at the rear of the tree stump were two of the worst kept men he had ever witnessed. Their long hair was tangled and matted, as was their long beards. The clothes they were wearing didn't look, or smell, like they had ever been washed, and they were not wearing any shoes on their grubby feet. The shorter of the two, with a mild hunch in his back, spat out words through the clump that was his beard.

"Why does the Mistress want us to mark this stump? We should set it afire, Morvran, and be done with it," says the miserable hunched man.

"Aye, Cradoc, I agree with ye, but if the Mistress learns of it, she will have our tongues, she will. Now go around to the front of this blasted stump and put her mark on the seat and let's be off. I'd like to fill me belly with some of that fine buck we took from here," spits out Morvran.

"Aye, right! As if there' be any left by the time we get back. You know what that lot is like with a bit of gristle. They'll eat the bones and all and leave us with nothing," says Cradoc, as he walks to the front of Grand Daddy.

Upon hearing that these mean men were to source of the poaching and the strange markings, he stands up on Grand Daddy's seat and yells out, "You, stop right there!" he yells in his most demanding voice.

Cradoc jumps back in fright, his pouch held up to cover his face. "Forgive me, Sire! I mean you no harm," he grovels, tears suddenly running down his face, mixing with the bit of food and dirt already trapped within his beard.

"Who are you that threatens us?" yells Morvran, coming up behind his companion.

He shoves Cradoc aside in disgust at the loudly weeping man and stands in front of Charles and Grand Daddy, baring his crossbow.

"This is my land, poacher! You are not welcome here. Leave now or be dealt with," challenges Charles.

"How will you do that, 'old man?' I see no weapons upon you. Maybe you will run us over with that loud contraption over there," he says, pointing to the Panther.

"No, you 'evil ones,' I have other ways to deal with your kind," says Charles.

Cradoc stepped back, a look of fear in his eyes. "He called us 'evil ones,' he knows!"

"Words mean nothing, Cradoc! They will not protect him from what I'm about to do to him," says Morvran, smiling wickedly, showing his black teeth through a dirty grey beard. He raises his crossbow to finish off this meddling old man.

"Morvran, look!" screams Cradoc, pointing to Lake Percival. "The Mist!" He turns to run, but his foot catches on a root of the tree stump and he falls, his pouch flying away into the nearby thickets that dot the lake shore.

Morvran turned, lowering his crossbow, and stared in disbelief at the gathering mist which seemed to emanate from the lake itself. "Let us depart this place, Cradoc. We will meet again, old man." With that last parting rant, the two unkempt men run off into the forest. Charles turned to step down from Grand Daddy when he saw the mist the two men mentioned coming from the Lake. "It seems we have a guardian, Grand Daddy. Aunt Josie was right after all. The mist is real! I must warn the family," he whispers to himself.

"Warn the family of what, Grampa?" asks Ken, who suddenly rounds the stump, surprising their grandfather.

"What the heck! Boys! You scared the daylights out of me!" he yells, still unsettled by his encounter with the poachers.

"Sorry, Grampa Charles! We didn't mean to scare you," says Griffin. "I thought the poachers had come back again; I smelled a foul stench back in the woods."

"Yeah, Grampa, we were worried something was heading your way," says Ken.

"There were two men, nasty pieces of work too, they tried to put that black shield symbol on Grand Daddy's seat, but I stopped them," says Charles.

"This must be theirs, then," says Griffin, swinging a small pouch in his hands. "I found this nasty, smelly thing in the thickets over by the lake shore. There's a few small brushes and a few sealed ceramic jars in it."

Charles took the pouch and taking in its contents, pulled the drawstring closed and handed it back to Griffin. "That belongs to the one I saw with a hunchback. He got scared and tried to run off but tripped over one of Grand Daddy's roots. I saw it go flying, but he was so scared he just got up and ran off into the woods," laughed Charles.

"What about the other one, Grampa?" asked Ken.

"The other one had the crossbow. The bolts we have been finding must be his. They also were the poachers we were looking for," says Charles. Griffin knew his Grampa wasn't telling the whole story, that something else had happened when they were almost to the Lake, but he was comforted that his Grampa felt he could be strong for them and knew that they would have his back if he needed it.

"We best get back to the house, boys. I have a story to tell, and the family must be present," says Charles. He patted Grand Daddy one more time and walked around to where the Panther was parked. Griffin stayed by Grand Daddy for a moment. He couldn't stop thinking about what the poachers were going to put on Grand Daddy. Standing there, his eyes became transfixed on the backrest of the stump, from which out of nowhere, a red dragon appeared, identical to the one on the gate. "No way!" he gasped. He held out his hands, as if the answers would appear there, and gaped at them. "Did I make that? How in the world could this have happened?"

"Griffin," yelled Charles, "Let's go, and toss that smelly thing into the woods."

Griffin looked at the small pouch and tossed it into the trees but made sure he knew where it was so he could find it later. He wanted to know more about those poachers, but now wasn't a good time, and he made no mention of the red dragon, or his newly awakened powers.

CHAPTER ELEVEN

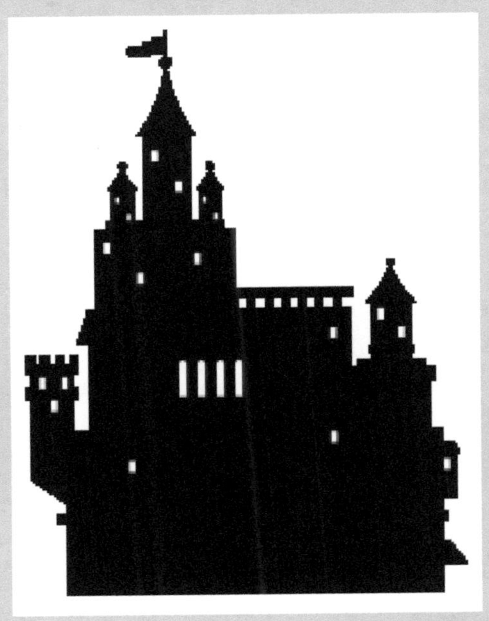

The castle keep was a foreboding place, heavy ramparts jutted into a cloudy expanse of sky. The few sparse trees surrounding the keep, and its village of huts, barely provided any cover from the ever-prevailing winds that whipped down from the Black Mountains. The cold was an ever-present reminder to the residents of the village that their duties to their Mistress and the Council of Elders were the only thing keeping them alive in the waste of the mountain's foothills.

In a room within the castle keep, there stood a large shield of black color with a bright red mark across its center. The shield a symbol of the dark power held by the castle's mistress, Morgan Le Fey, or Morgana. It's very essence one of darkness and dread.

Mistress Morgana sat in front of the fireplace; eyes locked on the flames as they danced upward into the chimney. The fire barely gave off enough warmth to heat the library. Its shelves of books, worn with age, only providing a paltry semblance of warmth to the room; and the broad windows looking out onto the mountains did not bring any warmth in with the sunlight. The long room was filled with heavy furniture and old, worn tapestries of battles long forgotten with a large fireplace at the back end, where the mistress resided, reading her correspondence. She sat huddled within the slim comfort of the old chairs that had resided in the library for untold years. She luxuriated in the warmth of the fire, and the quiet space the corralling chairs provided her. The hooded cloak she constantly wore provided enough warmth to sustain her, but the fire was a nice touch. She reached out toward the fire tossing a black powder into its flames. Watching the flames rise higher, she smiled at the fierce antics of the flames.

"Branwen is there anything that can be done to make this hideous chair more comfortable?" she asks, her maid looked over to her and said, "no Mistress, I'm sorry. It's seen better times, I'm afraid. I could get young Einion to make you a most comfortable lounge and it would be as comfortable as any throne," says Branwen, pulling strings from a sweater she was mending.

"That would be a lovely replacement, but you know as well as I that we can't afford to get soft right now," the Mistress said. Branwen continued to mend the sweater and watched closely as her mistress contemplated the letter in her hand, her brow increasingly becoming wrinkled as she shuffled within the chair. Finally, she threw the letter in the fire, sparking a range of emotions across her pale, narrow face, and turned to Branwen. "Branwen, this is unbearable. How is anyone to live with these conditions. I should never have accepted the Elders recommendation that this distasteful keep was a better rally point than my home by the sea."

"What if Einion were to make you a soft padded cushion for your chair? Surely,

that would help with the discomfort," asked Branwen, consolingly, seeing that her Mistress was in a dangerous mood. The Mistress sat up and looked around, seemingly forgetting her discomfort, "Have those two fools returned yet? I sent for them to be before me when they returned."

"Mistress?" inquired Branwen. She was not aware of any impending arrival of Charges, but Mistress did not aways provide the necessary information to her when she wanted something done. It just had to magically be done.

"I sent two fools on a mission to make a Fall and place a marker on that apparent throne." she grumbled, pushing the nonexistent padding around the barren chair.

"They returned a few minutes ago, Mistress. They probably are with the rest of the men, finishing off dinner. I will have Trystan fetch them for you," says Branwen.

"I have been sensing something strange recently," says the Mistress, as she pulls her robes more tightly about her. "None of the Charges have returned from their Falls with any sign of the strong bloodline that is supposedly still in that area, hopefully those two louts will have something for me," says the Mistress. She settles more firmly into the chair and welcomes the blanket that Branwen throws over her frame. "I could smell a strangeness about them, Branwen, but I paid it no mind. Most of the Charges return from a Fall with odors about them, but then they had a different aura about them that intrigued me. I must be certain. Was this the place that the strange feeling came from?"

Branwen listened to her Mistress before she stepped to the passageway to give the guard, Trystan, his orders. The Mistress was still ranting about lazy Charges and Branwen saw that leaving while the Mistress was talking could lead to harsh discipline, even to her Lady-in-waiting, so she hung back and responded to her Mistress as needed. There have been times when the Mistress would carry on talking to herself for hours, but thankfully, not this time.

"Yes, Bronwen, please tell Trystan to fetch them," says the Mistress.

Branwen stepped through the passage and approached Trystan. The tall, bearded man stood before the library doors, guarding the Mistress and the passage beyond. He stood alert at his post and smiled at Branwen as she approached.

"Good day, Trystan," said Branwen, smiling at the guard.

Trystan straightened himself even further when her heard her voice, which was warm and lovely. "At your service, Milady."

“The Mistress requests you to please fetch Morvran and Cradoc. It seems they have returned, but failed to report,” says Branwen, who frowned and almost made Trystan cry at her disappointment.

“Those two! They were just here, and then they walked off mumbling to themselves. Do not worry, Milady. I know their whereabouts. More than likely, they are in the kitchens having their fill of the larder and the Mistress’s stout beer,” says Trystan, chest puffed out at the boon of aiding such a lovely, young lady as Lady Branwen.

“Thank you, Trystan. Please inform me when they have arrived,” requests Branwen. Trystan watches as she returns through the passageway toward the library. He yearns for her favor, as did all the men. Her heart was a brilliant glow in the darkness, and her kindness was a gift she readily shared. He leaves his post and makes his way toward the kitchens.

Branwen returns to the library and her Mistress, wishing that it was a little warmer in the room. The meager rasher of wood wasn’t enough to warm anywhere else but by the fireplace, and she was not able to sit close to the fire as she was mending a shirt for one of the poor Charges. The windows the only other source of light in the room.

She waited by the entrance for the return of Trystan and the men requested by her Mistress. It wasn’t but a few minutes when Trystan entered the passageway, leading the two men behind him. “Milady, the two you have requested are waiting for her Mistress’s permission to enter,” says Trystan.

“Thank you, Trystan,” says Branwen. She enters the library and calls out to her Mistress, “Mistress, the two men you have requested are here.”

“Let them enter, Branwen,” says the Mistress, with a tired and bored sigh. She unwound herself from the blankets and rose to face the Charges before her. She held up a hand to her nose, trying to assuage the stench coming off of the two unwashed men.

Morvran and Cradoc entered from the passageway with heads bowed to pay reverence to the Mistress. “Mistress, the two you requested have arrived,” said Branwen. She watched as the Mistress languidly stalked toward the two shivering men. A wicked, slightly insane, smile slashed across her face, making her normally placid features appear demonic. Branwen had witnessed the Mistress’s anger, her ability to inflict pain, even death at times, when she loses control of her anger. The

Mistress stood and waved her right arm, both men dropped to their knees. They tried to speak but were rendered mute by her magic.

"Why have you fools not reported directly to me when you arrived back? Is it not an easy thing to do?" she asked, not expecting answers from the two silent men, she walked over to the older man. "Morvran, what have you to say for yourself?"

Gasping at the sudden ability to speak, he could barely utter his words as he looked up at her beautiful, but terrible, countenance. "An evil man was lying in wait, Mistress. He called the mist on us before we could complete our mission. We had to flee. Apologies, Mistress!" says Morvran, cowering on the floor before her.

"The mist? Who was this man?" asks the Mistress, her anger rising as quickly as her voice. She had never heard of the Charges encountering the mist. This made her nervous, and frustrated, never a good combination at any time.

"I know not, Mistress," croaked out Morvran.

"Cradoc, do you have anything to report?" she asks, not expecting anything from the sobbing man at her feet. He struggled to gather himself and spoke hesitantly, "Yes, Mistress. I was about to put the markings on the stump when this very tall man stood from inside it. He ordered me to stop, even though he was unarmed," says Cradoc, groveling at her feet.

"Stand Cradoc, so I may not strain my neck speaking to you,' says the Mistress, disdainfully.

Cradoc glanced uncertainly at Morvran, who was still on his knees. He was confused and scared. Normally, Morvran does all the talking when they report to the Mistress. Cradoc shakily stands submissively in front of his Mistress while gesturing toward Morvran, who was kneeling quietly on the floor, "we asked this man who he was, and he said 'this is my land poacher. You are not welcome here. He told us to leave or be dealt with severely." His head still bowed, he stood in front of the Mistress, hoping that he would not be set on fire.

"Morvran, do you agree with Cradoc's story," she looks at the man, expectantly. He rubs his neck nervously, "yes, Mistress. The mist was floating just above the lake, like it was coming up from the very bottom, and moving toward us. Please forgive our cowardice, Mistress."

Mistress Morgana gestures for the two men to go, no longer able to tolerate their stench and appearance. "I will not forget your actions, but I will be lenient, this

time," says the Mistress, as she smiles sweetly at them. "For your actions, I forbid you to enjoy any fruits of your actions upon the lands of the foreign world. You will also spend time in my garden of thorns, tending to my treasures, making sure they are healthy and sharp, without the aid of gloves, I think. Do you understand?" demands the Mistress.

"Yes, Mistress," they respond. Though, Cradoc is still a nervous, sobbing mess as he turns to leave.

"Be warned, you will be monitored, do not slack on any tasks, or I will be made aware, and the punishment shall be severe," the Mistress Morgana warns.

"Yes, Mistress," agree the two men, bowing as they back away from the terrible presence that is their Mistress. She turns away from the two fleeing men, happy with the spike of fear she induced within the men. She walks back through the library, frustrated at the lack of warmth, and the many dusty books surrounding her. As she walks past a reading table she pushes a stack of books petulantly off onto the floor, not caring for the destruction or the importance of the books. She sits and allows the warmth of the fire to placate her fractious moods, "I suppose Einion can see if he can make a cushion that would please me, Branwen," says Mistress Morgana. "If it wasn't for their encounter with the mist, I would have taken an ear from each of them, stupid fools."

Branwen sits down at the reading table after picking up the stack of books the Mistress tossed onto the floor and picks up her mending. "Mistress shows great restraint. They will forever be grateful for your generosity. I'm curious though, if I may, Mistress. Why would they not be used to seeing this mist when on a Fall?" Though she knows the opportunity to see any signs of the mist are near impossible now and have been for years.

"Never has a Charge seen the mist on a Fall to the future, not in many years. I have seen it many times when I was younger, but that was many years ago, and I have lost the ability to see it now," the Mistress laments, sadly.

"Why now though, if the mist hasn't been seen in many years, Mistress?" asks Branwen, quietly.

"The one they said called the mist says he has control over those lands. This tells me that the bloodline has been found, and that they are getting stronger. If that is so, then we must be very cautious when next anyone makes a Fall. I must check my books, maybe there is more information about this particular bloodline in one of the old journals. Branwen, tell Trystan I am not do be disturbed for the rest of the evening," says Mistress Morgana. Branwen moves to obey the orders, but her Mistress's voice calls out again, "One other thing, my beautiful Branwen, do tell the Elders that there will be no further Falls until I am satisfied that we will not be stepping into a trap. You are to seal the cave till I give the word," orders Mistress Morgana.

"Immediately, Mistress," says Branwen, running out of the library, her darning materials in her arms.

CHAPTER TWELVE

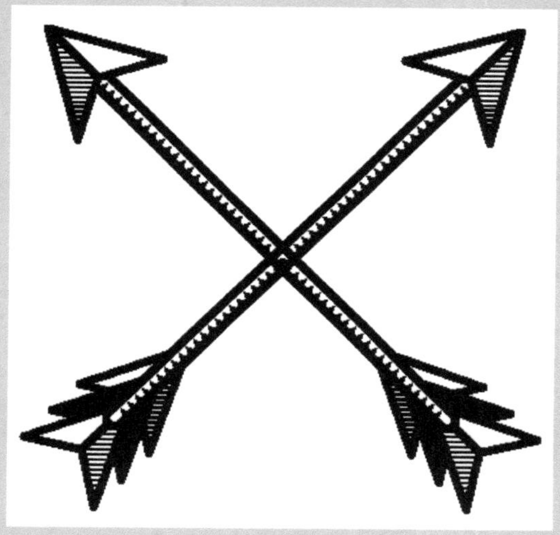

The sun was just about to go behind the barn when Amelia and Gavin decided to take a break on the porch swing, and have some iced tea, relaxing in the late afternoon sunlight. The breeze was mild, making the heat of the June day temperate.

"Today was a perfect day for making sun tea," said Gavin. "Not a cloud in the sky, my favorite girl by my side," he hugs Amelia closer to himself, "and our boys are doing great."

"Don't forget that there's an adventure mystery afoot, Sweetheart," teased Amelia.

"Can't forget about that. I'm sure when they get back Griffin will have plenty of stories to tell about Knights and secret plans to take over the homestead," he laughs. Amelia, sipping her tea, agrees, "I bet he will."

"The tea is very good, Hun," says Gavin as he leans in and gives Amelia's cheek a small peck. He is always pleased to see that she still blushes after over 20 years of marriage.

"Thank you," Amelia takes her due with grace.

"When did Gwen and Sayer say they would get here?" asked Gavin.

"About eight o'clock because Sayer wasn't able to get off work until 6," says Amelia, "They should be here soon."

"That does not give him much time to get cleaned up after work, and it takes them about an hour to drive here," says Gavin.

"Yeah, I said that too, but Gwen said she was going to save some time by having the kids eat supper early, around five, hopefully saving some time that way and Sayer will have time to clean up. You know how long it takes small children to be ready to go anywhere," she smiles at the memory of a small Griffin and the wailing he would make when they had to get dressed for an outing.

Gavin looked out toward the north pasture hoping that no more poaching would be done on their land. He would hate to have to stop the boys' wandering ways, especially as this was Ken's last summer before college. "Dad still hasn't said why he wanted the whole family here. It's not like him to miss supper. Has he come out to eat since they got back?" Gavin was worried about his father.

"Not yet. I knocked on his door a little bit ago and asked if he was okay, and he said he was fine," says Amelia.

"Where are the boys now?" asks Gavin.

"Kenrich went to the shed. He said one of the Panther's tires needed some air, and Griffin's in his room, playing on his tablet, like normal," she said, chuckling. She overheard him talking to his friend Own when she went to check on him after supper. He was energetically telling his friend about what they had found this afternoon.

"Did Griff say anything else about the drawing on the gate?" he asked.

"Not a word. He said that Charles said not to say anything until the whole family has arrived," she said.

"Well, we'll know soon enough. The Jones family has finally arrived," says Gavin in anticipation. A SUV comes up the driveway to the house, and parks. Inside they can hear voices and shouts of excitement coming from their grandchildren. Amelia and Gavin greet their daughter Gwen and her husband Sayer as they come up the steps. Gwen leads the way with Sayer, holding one year old Alan in one arm while a happily chattering three-year-old Dylan holds his other hand.

"Hi, mom and dad," says Gwen, giving them both a one arm hug, passing the baby over to her father, who began making funny faces at him, making his laugh loudly.

"Hi kids, sorry for this short notice, but Grampa Charles insisted that you were here for his announcement," says Amelia, as she bends down to pick up Dylan, who is jumping up and down screaming to be picked up. "Oh, right. No need to scream, baby."

"We're about to find out, but first let me have this fine young man you're hauling around, Gavin," she says, as they pass a child between them. The children settle down in the arm of their grandparents, babbling about the bug they saw or the ice cream they ate last night for dinner.

They put the children down as they embraced each other properly. "Gramma!" yelled Alan, the baby just learning how to talk and insistent at being held at all times. Kay was standing next to Gavin with her tail wagging, while licking Dylan's face. Letting go of his dad's hand, he embraced her head, which made her tail wag harder.

"Looks like he's gonna be busy for a while," says Sayer, motioning toward the dog and boy now sitting in a pile on the porch.

"That it does, now let's all go into the family room and have a seat. I'll get the boys and Charles in here. If anyone wants refreshments, help yourself, we have some nice, iced tea made this afternoon. Hun, you want to fill them in on what happened this afternoon?" asks Amelia, as she headed up the stairs to get the others.

The family room in the Defaid house was, as its name implies, large enough to hold the whole family. It was the place everyone went after holiday meals, or just to be together on an evening night. It has a fireplace, two large couches and two big easy chairs, filled with comfortable throw pillows and a few blankets for cold winter days, all showing their use after years of lovely care. Pictures of the family hung on one wall, and up the staircase, and above the fireplace were three crossbows hung together with a plaque with the family motto, 'Byth Heb,' in Welsh.

"Yeah, what is this all about?" ask Gwen, trying to wrangle a squirmy Dylan into sitting between his parents.

Just then, Ken steps into the room, "Hi, Gwen," bending down to give her a hug, "I think we should wait for Grampa before we discuss anything."

"None of us are sure of what this is all about, but this is what went on this morning," says Gavin, filling in Gwen and Sayer the news of what happened this morning in the north by the lake.

A couple minutes went by, and Griffin entered the family room carrying the book of heraldry. "Hi, everybody! How are you guys doing?" he asks as he side hugs his sister and sits down between the two, opening the book for Dylan to look at the brightly colored pictures.

"We're doing fine, Griff. How have you been? I've heard you had quite the adventure this morning," says Sayer.

"Pretty good, Uncle Sayer," says Griffin.

"I see you still keep up with the heraldry and the medieval stuff. Does that have something to do with this little get-together?" asks Gwen.

"It surely does," responds Charles as he enters the family room with a cold glass of iced tea, carrying Aunt Josie's journal in his other hand. Amelia follows behind him, a rowdy Alan in her arms, carrying two sippy cups for the children in her other hand.

Once everyone has been welcomed, Charles looks around for his oldest great-grand child, Dylan, "Where's the oldest one of yours gotten off too?"

"He's outside now, Grampa, playing with Kay. I can fetch him if you want?" says Sayer.

"Oh no, that's okay. I'll get to see him later. I'd take young Alan from Amelia, but I see he has fallen asleep. Must have been that car ride. If I remember correctly, his mother will always fall asleep in the car," chuckles Charles, looking to Gwen and sharing a smile.

"Yeah, he does get that from me, alright," she says.

Charles took a seat in the one of the remaining chairs and sits back for a second, taking in his surrounding family. Glad that he has this time with them. The warmth of the evening and the familiar voices make his certainty about what he is about to share more relevant.

"Grampa, please tell us what this is about. The boys should have been in bed a while ago now," says Gwen.

"I know, Gwen, and this won't take long, but with events happening today, I felt I must not remain silent any longer. The family deserves to know about our history, to protect us," says Charles, gravely. They all look at him in shock, except the boys, they have seen the evidence of something strange stirring in the woods. Charles puts the old leather journal down on the coffee table between them and unties the leather strap, unwrapping the protective outer layer. He reveals a layer of green leather inside the old leather covering. Printed on the cover were the words, 'Byth Heb.'

I'm sorry for calling you all together at this late hour, but what I am about to tell you can't wait any longer," he says. He picks up the journal and held it up so all could see it. "What I have here is the 'Defaid Family Journal.' It was passed on to me in 1980 by my Great Aunt Josephine, or Aunt Josie, as we all called her back then. She was sister to my Great Grandfather Maxen Llacheu Defaid. Her father, Derwin Llacheu Defaid, died of a stroke in 1900, and as the oldest of the family bloodline, she was given the task of preserving the history of our family, which she did for 80 years."

"Why haven't we seen this family journal before now, Dad?" asked Gavin.

"I asked Aunt Josie that very same question, and her answer was that it was for our protection. This isn't the first written history of the Defaid family, Gavin. The first was lost in the fire of 1870. That one had a detailed history going back hundreds of years. Stories of our Welsh forefathers. A few pages were able to be saved, but sadly, many of those stories were lost in the fire. This later version was started in 1870, shortly after the fire. Our family entered what they could remember of the stories from the original family journal, but to someone who does not know the real truth about what is written on these pages, it is like reading a fantasy story," says Charles, putting the journal down on the coffee table again.

"Protection from what exactly, Grampa?" asks Gwen.

Charles leans forward in his chair, "An evil that has plagued our family for nearly fifteen hundred years, my child," he says to his surrounding family. The room began to fill with mutterings of astonishment, and then a silence fell over everyone, all eyes focusing on Charles.

"As you all know, this morning when I was checking the fence line, I came across a strange shield with a red chevron across its center. I thought at first it was Griffin putting medieval drawings on the fence, but I was wrong," he says, Griffin shakes his head in agreement. "Griff, show everyone the picture you have in your book," asks Charles.

Griffin opened his book of heraldry to the page with the picture of a black shield, red chevron, and three red dragons on it. "That's not the same as the one Charles described being on the fence, but it is alarmingly close," said Amelia, leaning closer to the book to get a better look.

"Yeah, I know, Mom. That's why I wanted to look at it in person," says Griffin.

"Whose coat of arms is this one, then, Griffin?" asks Gwen.

"Morgan Le Fey, also known as Morgana the Enchantress," says Griffin.

"So, what did the one on the gate look like to you, Griff?" asks Sayer.

"By the time we got there someone had painted a red dragon over it," says Griffin. This time everyone spoke at once. The room filled with voices asking questions that no one had any real answers to.

Griffin stood up and opened the book, showing a red dragon emblazoned on the page. "This was painted over the black and red shield. It is the red dragon on the flag of Wales. It stands for valor and bravery."

"Who is doing this, Dad? First the poaching on our land, now these things painted on our gate?" asks Gavin, frustrated and a little frightened for his family.

"When I saw the bolts that Ken had found, I remembered seeing that kind before. One was given to me by Aunt Josie when she passed the Family journal on to me. Her father found it embedded in the back of his brother, Teghan, during the fire of 1870," says Charles.

"Wasn't he found in the house after the fire was put out?" asked Amelia.

"That is what you all have been told. The truth is he was found on the steps leading to the mud room of the kitchen, where the fire started. It is believed he was trying to get into the house to put out the fire when he was shot and killed. His mother Jenna, and Grandmother Eres, were both on the front porch and didn't know of the fire till it was too late to put it out," says Charles. His expression is suddenly grim, "Let me make this short. We are hunted by 'evil ones' who can travel forward in time and space. Their purpose is to control the spread of our bloodline."

"Why now? Couldn't they have done this a long time ago?" asks Ken.

"They thought they had when Teghan was murdered. He was the one in our bloodline that had the special powers to drive the evil ones away," says Charles.

Ken sits forward on the edge of the couch, looking earnestly at his Grampa, 'Was that the powers that scared the poachers away today? Grampa, are you the one in our bloodline with the special powers now?"

"I don't know," says Charles, "I never felt any more different then, than I do now."

"You saw the poachers?" asks Gavin, sitting up quickly, almost knocking the drinks off the coffee table.

"This is really hard to believe, Grampa!" says Gwen, clearly alarmed and worried about her children. She stood and took a sleeping Alan from Amelia's arms. "Excuse me for a few minutes. I'm going to fetch Dylan and try to get them to sleep in Mom and Dad's room for a bit."

"You stay here, Gwen," Sayer says as he reaches for the sleepy Alan, "I'll take care of the boys. This is stuff you need to hear. You can fill me in later, okay?"

"Okay, but it is confusing me," says Gwen, sitting back down on the couch after

releasing Alan.

Charles gives Gwen a quick reassuring smile and continues his story. “Yes, there were two of them. One was a medium height and build, while the other shorter one had a hunchback. At first, I thought they were just poachers, but then I heard one of them tell the other to put the Mistress’s mark on the seat of Grand Daddy. That is when I called them ‘evil ones’ and told them to leave or they would be dealt with harshly. The one with the crossbow aimed it at me, but before he could do more than threaten me with it, the other one saw the mist. They both ran away into the forest in fright at that.”

CHAPTER THIRTEEN

"When Ken and I were returning to Grampa, I saw a bit of mist form on the lake, but I thought it was just evening fog," says Griffin. He didn't want anyone to know about his powers. He was afraid they might think he was just playing up into the adventure of it all.

"Let me get this straight. You're saying we have these powers, and that there are those that come from another time to control those of us who have these powers?" asked an incredulous Gavin.

"Yes, Gavin, I am. Aunt Josie told me, and her father told her. This has been passed down for hundreds of years," says Charles, looking at his son's disbelieving face.

"But I still don't understand why we weren't told all of this till now, Dad!" says Gavin.

"To protect us from the 'evil ones,' as they are called in the journal. Remember that a lot of our family history was lost when the first journal was destroyed. Even the name 'Defaid' is not our original true name. The journal mentions that it was changed from Llacheu to Defaid in the early 1700's, sometime before coming to Canada, or so it was believed," explains Charles.

"So, they thought they could hide us from the 'evil ones?'" asks Gwen.

"Yes, I guess they did, but that was a long time ago. It seems that the power within our bloodline has been felt by the 'evil ones' when it is at its strongest. The journal says that our forebears have learned that much at least. That's another reason to keep this a secret. The less people know about our family history, the better," says Charles.

"But, if these powers are so powerful, and the 'evil ones can sense when they grow in strength, why all the secrecy?" asked Gwen.

"Family history has told me that the 'evil ones' want to use our power, that they can sense when it is at its strongest. We have been kept safe over the years, by keeping a low profile, and the fact that the 'evil ones' cannot directly find us. It is as if we are warded," says Charles.

"Is that what the poachers were doing? Trying to find the source of the powers?" asks Ken.

"I'm not sure, Ken, but that might explain why they painted those markings on the gate, as a sign that something of interest was in the area," says Charles.

As Griffin sat and listened to his family, he was filled with regrets in his heart. He wanted to share what he had learned about himself with his family and help them understand better, but he needed more time. More time to figure his new abilities out himself.

“Then who painted over the black and red shield with the red dragon, then?” asks Amelia.

“That is where the story in the journal gets a bit sketchy. Our forebears wrote very little about where our powers originated. One journal entry mentions a seeker, who sent squires to help with the harvest. Another says, ‘The need for the stone has passed. The family order has returned.’ Even Aunt Josie wasn’t sure what that meant,” says Charles.

Griffin had to say something. He had been too quiet, listening. “It must have been put there by our Welsh ancestors. I mean, who else would know about this.”

“What about that nasty smell, Grampa?” asks Ken. “I didn’t smell anything like that when I found the deer, nor when Dad and I went to fetch it.”

“That had to be the two ‘evil ones’ we saw. I could smell them when they approached Grand Daddy,” says Charles.

“Yea, that pouch I found smelled nasty too!” says Griffin, in excitement.

“What pouch was that?” asks Gavin.

“The smaller one with the hunched back tripped as he was running away, and it went flying into the grass near the lake shore. Griffin found it in the brush,” said Charles.

“It smelled bad, and the inside was a mess of red and black paint splotches all over it. There were two brushes and small sealed jars. They must have been holding some kind of paint. It was nasty!” says Griffin, making a disgusted face at the memory of the nasty smells.

“Any idea where they went, Dad?” asked Gavin.

“They were headed west into the forest. When I faced the lake, I saw a white mist floating about it, and in the next moment the boys returned,” says Charles.

“What’s with this mist, Grampa?” asks Gwen.

"I'm not sure, Gwen, but Aunt Josie told me the mist is a good thing, and a guardian of our family and lands. It is also mentioned in the journal by her grandfather, Eric Llacheu," Charles says, holding up the journal to the page that mentions the strange mist. Everybody takes a turn looking over the pages, murmurs spread among those sitting around the coffee table.

"What are we to do, Charles?" asks Amelia.

"Go on with our lives but be watchful. They know there is something here now, but not exactly what or who. I do believe we are protected for the time being, because someone painted a red dragon over the other symbol."

"Can I take this home with me tonight? I would really like to study it," asks Gwen.

"I'm sorry, Gwen, but it must stay with me. I am its keeper and must keep it here for the family to read. I keep it in my fire safe for protection. Just ask me when you come the next time and I'll be happy to get it for you to read," says Charles.

"Thanks, Grampa," says Gwen. She stands, as the conversation seems to be dwindling now, and heads for the bedroom to retrieve her two sleepy children. Sayer gathers the children's toys and gets ready for the long drive home. Ken asks his Grampa, "Do we still keep it a secret?"

"Yes, Ken, most definitely! We do not tell anyone from this day on. Not even the little ones, Dylan and Alan, are to know unless it is necessary. I tell you now because of the danger current events mean for our family. We would also be considered insane if this was to become common knowledge. The word would spread and 'evil ones' would have no trouble locating us. As it stands right now, they may already know," says Charles. "Also, keep in mind that if something were to happen to me, this journal goes to the next oldest of our family. That means Gavin would take it next then Gwen, then Ken, and then Griffin," says Charles.

Gwen and Sayer promised to come visit with the kids next weekend. Amelia and Gavin gave the kids hugs and walked them out to their car. After they drove away, the rest of the family settled onto the porch, exhausted from the tale told to them. Griffin said good night to his mom and dad and went up to get ready for bed.

CHAPTER FOURTEEN

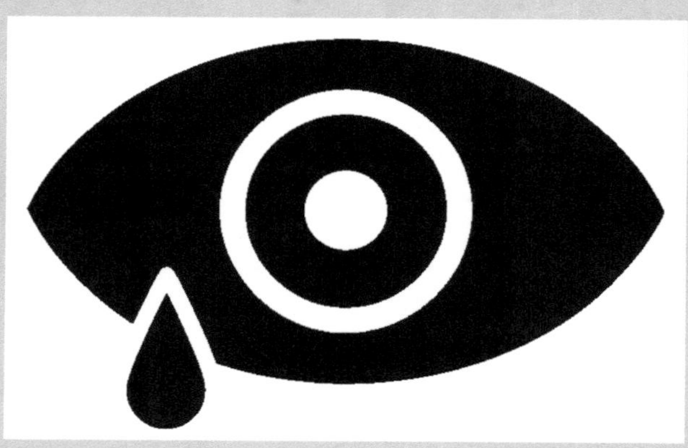

"What are you trying to tell me, Cradoc?" Branwen said, seeing the fear in his eyes.

"I've lost my pouch, Milady. I lost it on my last Fall," he says, as he wrings his hand in agitation.

He looked at the ground too ashamed to look up into the light of Lady Branwen's face.

"Cradoc, that was over a month ago now, what have you been doing since, and why are you telling me this now?" she asks.

"I've been working in Mistress's Garden of Thorns until just last week, Milady. I did not need my pouch until now, so I didn't know it was missing. Please, Milady, I need the pouch if I was to make another Fall," he cried piteously.

"Why not have the saddlers make you a new one?" she asks.

"The Elders inspect the logbooks every day. They would surely find out and I would be punished. Please, Milady, I need your help!" he says. Branwen looked down at the wretched man, his weeping tugging at her heart. She was conflicted. She didn't want to see him get punished for such a trivial thing as losing his work pouch, but it wasn't her place to go and ask for another one to be made, not without someone asking questions. The Mistress would surely find out from one of the Elders that she had procured the pouch without authorization.

"Why have you come to me for help?" she asks.

Cradoc lifted his head and looked into Branwen's soft brown eyes and his face filled with crushing hopefulness. "We know you are of a good spirit, Milady. You have always been there for us Charges. If you say no, then I will not ask again, but Milady, you can make a Fall without an Elder's aid. You are the only one who can open the cave. No one will know, Milady, if we do it now, when the Falls are halted. Please, Milady, I beg of you!"

Branwen looked down at the hunched man, his pleading taking root in her heart. "Go to the Well of Healing and hide behind it till I summon you."

"But, Milady, the Well of Healing!" he squeaked in fear.

"Do not be frightened, Cradoc. You will not be healed today for your misdeeds," she says.

"Oh, thank you, Milady. May the God's light shine upon you this day," he said and scurried away.

Branwen continued her stroll up the path from the village to her hut in the southern part of the town. It was nearing late afternoon when she arrived home. It had been a long day dealing with the petulant demands of the Mistress, who had her tending to her pet tiger-tail lizard all day. It had been acting strangely lately, and now she knew why. She had been sent with his handler into the forest to find the herbs needed to calm him. He was experiencing anxiety from being taken away from the swamps of Laurylen. She sat down on the stool in her small kitchen, she sighed into her teacup, steam rising from the vessel as she contemplated her next actions.

It had been an hour since Cradoc had left Branwen and he was slumped down behind the dreaded Well of Healing. He was shifting into a more comfortable position when he heard voices coming from the pathway outside the chamber. Stilling, he listened.

"This is not a good idea, Gerallt. If the Elders learn of this we'll not walk away from here," the voice belonged to Rhain, another of Cradoc's Charge.

"Look, my friend, he must answer for his shameful deeds. You know as well as I do that the Elders will not raise a hand against one of their own," said Gerallt, his nasally voice penetrating the chamber where Cradoc hid.

"What if we could ask to talk to the Mistress?" asked Rhain.

"Don't be a fool, Rhain! She would have our tongues just for speaking ill of one of the Elders," spat Gerallt.

"Let us talk to the Lady Branwen, then. She always has an ear for us Charges, and she might be able to talk to the Mistress on our behalf," said Rhain.

"No, Rhain! We cannot take the chance. No one must know of our plot to get rid of Elder Macsen. No matter how it is done, it must be done! His cruelty toward us Charges has gone on long enough. It wasn't so bad when we had the Falls to keep the Elders busy, but now that they have halted, we are stuck with Elder Macsen's insanity," says Garallt.

"Yes, you are right Gerallt, and his madness has gotten worse since the halting of the Falls. Just this morning I heard he beat young Pedre for dropping a spoon when cleaning a table in the Elder's dining hall," the mention of the punishment caused both men to be silent for a moment.

"Let us be off for now, Rhain. We will make our final plans tomorrow," says Gerallt, walking away, Rhain trailing behind him.

Cradoc waited till their voices were fading away before peeking over the top of the Well, looking toward the chamber entrance for any sign or sound. He knew both men from previous Falls they had all been on with Morvran. Both were good men, but he didn't like the idea of an Elder being murdered. He knew that Elder Macsen could be cruel and quick tempered, but he was not too bad, most of the time. The men must have a good reason for their animosity toward the Elder.

"I must tell Morvran of this!" he says to himself.

"Tell Morvran of what?" says Branwen, startling the man as she approached the Well.

"Oh, my Lady, you startled me. Nothing, Milady, just some needed dusting that needs to be done in here. Very dusty," he says, wiping off the top of the Well with his sleeve.

"I saw Gerallt and Rhain just now in passing, they were mumbling something about Elder Macsen, did you hear anything while you were here, Cradoc?" she asks curiously.

"No, no, Milady, not a word, just whispers, I heard, Milady," he stutters out.

She put her hand onto his shoulder, giving it a comforting squeeze. "Listen to me, Cradoc. I cannot help you if you are not completely honest with me. Do you understand?"

Her touch calming him, he grudgingly admits, "Milady, they were talking about how cruel Elder Macsen has been since the Falls have been halted. They have reached the point where they cannot take any more!"

"Did they say what they were going to do?" she asks, worried for the man and his other Charges should anything be done to the Elder.

Cradoc could not look her in the eye, gazing at the ground. "They say he must die, Milady!" he whispered.

She gasped, putting her hand over her heart, which was beating fast. "No! They cannot do such a thing. I must warn Elder Macsen!"

"Please, Milady, talk to the men first, they will listen to your good counsel. They are good men, as you know. Something has to have happened to make this rash decision. I overheard them say the Elder punished a Charge this morning for dropping a spoon during cleanup." That seems a bit harsh, don't you believe, Milady," he rushes to say, worried about punishment, not just for the two men, but for all of them.

"I will talk to them tomorrow, as they are now out gathering. Come, Cradoc, we must retrieve your pouch quickly, before we are both missed," says Branwen.

"Yes, Milady. I overheard them say that they would make a final decision tomorrow, so it is good of you, Milady," he says.

"Do no worry yourself, Cradoc, for I have a plan. Now let's be off."

The chamber that held the Well of Healing sat near the border of the keep aligned with the forest. They took a path through the trees that led them to a deep crag of ancient stone monoliths, hidden by a large stone overhang concealed by a considerable amount of rock and debris leading into a system of caves. They stepped into the nearest, and largest cave, walking toward the back. Branwen lifted her hand into the air and whispered words of enchantment. The rock wall shimmered as she finished her spell. "Hold my hand," she says to Cradoc.

Gripping her hand like a vice, he lets her lead him into the shimmer and they make their Fall.

CHAPTER FIFTEEN

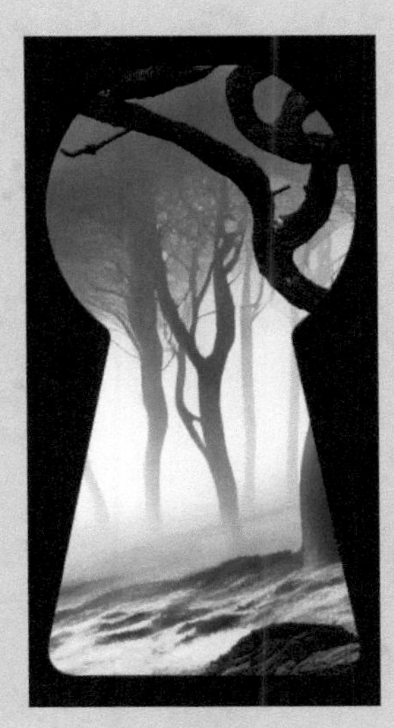

“It’s been almost five weeks since Grampa chased of the poachers, Dad. Let me go up to Grand Daddy and take a look around. There might be something new up there, and I miss the fishing,” sighed Ken. The long summer days had blended into July. It was almost time for him to start getting ready for college, and even though he was looking forward to it, he was interested to find out anything further about the family’s secrets.

“I don’t know, Ken. There could be all kinds of strange things going on up there. Maybe you should wait till I’m free, later this afternoon, and I’ll go with you,” suggested his dad.

“I won’t stay long, promise, and I’ll take Kay along with me for protection,” he said, looking down at the dog, who was nosing a lizard along with her nose. Ken sheepishly looked at his dad, “well, some protection. She did warn me of that black bear out near the Lake last year.”

“Hmm, I don’t know,” his dad smirked, “Okay, but take the radio, you know there’s zero cell reception out there. Call me when you get there and every fifteen minutes. It’s going to be dark soon, so don’t stay out too long, you hear?”

“Yes, Dad, thanks, Dad!” yells out Ken, running to the barn to get the Panther ready to go, Kay chasing behind him, excited to be going with him.

Griffin watched from his bedroom window as Ken drove off in the Panther. He had heard every word they had spoken. Ever since he had been accepted, his senses had become very keen. He could hear voices from quite a distance away, especially when he would focus hard. It did take him a few days to gain control over the background noise that always surrounded him, but he slowly gained an upper hand and now could hear a pin drop through a thunderstorm. He knew his brother would be okay going up to Grand Daddy. For over a month now, secretly, he had been exploring the area near the Lake and up Dee Run, honing his skills. Except for the evidence of the pouch, which was still hidden by the scrub near the lake shore, there had been no more evidence of poachers or evil ones around the farm.

He finished playing Star Gander with Owen, “Look, I gotta go. I’ll play again tomorrow, same time,” he waved at his friend and set his tablet down. He headed downstairs and passing through the family room, saw that Grampa Charles was watching an old western on the TV.

“Where are you off to, young man?” asks Charles.

“Oh, hi Grampa Charles. I didn’t see you there,” says Griffin, feigning ignorance.

‘Yeah, I see. You look in a big hurry. What Cha up too?”

“Nothing really, I’m going to check out the barn, there’s new kittens.”

“Better put on a sweater, you know how your mom is.”

“But, Grampa, it’s so hot outside!”

“I know, but humor me, son.”

“Okay, Grampa,” says Griffin, grabbing a light sweater off of the hook by the front door. He bounded down the from steps toward the barn. He knew the hayloft would be a good place to listen from, and there were kittens after all. He climbed into the hayloft and opened the doors that faced the north of the property. He could see far into the north pasture and just a glint of the Lake in the distance.

He sat down on a hay bale and watched as Ken and Kay left the south pasture and headed toward Lake Percival. He knew Ken had reached Grand Daddy when the Panther went silent. He listened intently for a whisper of a voice, meaning his hearing was getting more attuned to distance hearing.

“Well, Kay, what you say we go for a walk, and check things out,” asks Ken.

They passed Grand Daddy and followed Dee Run up to the Bathing Stone. “I guess this is far enough, Kay. No sign of any poachers so far or of any strange mist. Let’s head back to the Lake and have a seat on Grand Daddy.”

They slowly walked down the path, listening to the burble of Dee Run and enjoying the breeze through the trees. Summer had just peaked, and the heat was intense, it was nice to have the cool breeze off the stream for company. Suddenly, Kay growled lowly in her throat.

Ken turned quickly and kneeled facing Kay. “What is it, girl? Do you smell something?” Kay’s nose was raised as if she detected something intriguing, then she sneezed as if something foul was nearby. “Wow, that’s nasty!” says Ken, catching a hint of a pungent unpleasant smell, along with something light and floral. As suddenly as the smells appeared, they were gone. The wind shifting just enough so all he could smell now was lake. He looked at Kay, surprised that she was just sitting at his feet, tongue sticking out happily.

Griffin had also stood at Kay's sudden growl. It was distant, but he could still hear her rumble, even hundreds of yards away. He wanted to investigate that area in the morning, after chores.

"What's this, Kay? It's a red dragon symbol on the backrest of Grand Daddy," Ken says as he rounds the throne. "This must have been put on by those that painted that one on the gate." Griffin smiled to himself, knowing he was the one responsible for that symbol.

Ken sat on Grand Daddy and looked out over the still lake. Kay jumped up next to him on the bench seat. She suddenly sat up and began sniffing at the air as she had done earlier, but with no growling. "What is it, Kay? If it's that nasty smell again, I don't smell anything right now." At first, all he could smell was the damp earth, lake water, and growing plants, but as he stood, he caught an aroma that wasn't like anything he had ever experienced before. "Wow, Kay, what is that smell, it is amazing! Where is it coming from, do you think?" He got up and ran around to the other side of Grand Daddy and searched the surrounding area, not finding the source of that wonderful aroma.

Branwen had sensed they were not alone as they searched for Cradoc's missing pouch near the lake. As soon as it was found, she sent Cradoc back to the cave to wait for her. She would stay and see what had alerted her senses so much. She didn't have to wait long when she spied Ken and Kay coming down the path toward the lake. She froze momentarily as she saw a beautiful young man approach a large tree stump.

"He is so fair," she says softly. "I mustn't get too close, but how I want to bask in his beauty."

She moved forward and hid behind a large oak tree. At this angle she could get a better view of his face. She saw him turn to face her and started to race away.

"Hello, there," Ken said quickly, not daring to move forward for fear she would disappear. "You can come out from behind that tree. We don't bite," indicating himself and Kay. His senses said that she was not a threat.

Branwen stood motionless, caught in his hypnotic gaze. She stumbled and wished to run back toward the cave, but she also didn't sense any threat from the young man nor his dog. Slowly, she moved from behind the tree. Her long auburn hair blowing with the breeze.

Ken could not believe the vision he was looking at. He was enraptured by her

beauty. Pale, almost translucent skin and a fine, willowy figure, she was a dream come to life. "My name is Kenrich. What is yours, if I may know?"

Branwen heard him speak but was still caught up in his spell. "Branwen, my name is Branwen, Sir."

Ken saw that she was afraid to come closer, as she hesitated when she saw Kay. "This is my friend, Kay."

Suddenly, she remembered why she was here and the urgency of her mission. "I must go! I cannot be missed!" For a brief moment, she stared at his face, memorizing it, then raced away through the forest, disappearing from their view.

"Please, don't go!" yelled out Ken.

Griffin could feel his brother's sudden desperate cry. He also felt a new emotion that he could not name, but it seemed like a good thing to have. Then he heard faintly, a woman's voice calling out, longing could be heard in her voice, as she called out to Ken, that she must go, and he could sense how sad that made his brother feel.

Griffin wasn't positive, but he thought the name, Branwen, was familiar. He took the notepad he always kept with him and wrote it down for later investigation. He wasn't sure this would be a good time to question Ken about the mystery women, he still didn't know of Griffin's new powers or their extent. He would search around Grand Daddy tomorrow. If he finds anything interesting, or not, he will talk to his brother.

The cave was dark and very damp when she arrived back at the entrance. She left the warmth of the forest and looked around for her missing Charge, Cradoc. "Where are you, Cradoc?"

"Here, Milady." He popped up near the back of the cave, nervously waiting next to the shimmering wall.

"Were you able to find you missing items, Cradoc?"

"All but one brush, Milady, which can easily be replaced by catching a squirrel, Milady."

"Why do you need to capture a squirrel?"

"For its fur, Milady. The tail makes a great brush, very soft, Milady."

“Is there not another animal that would suit your needs more, Cradoc?”

“No, milady. There are not many in the area anymore, Milady. I have to go well beyond the keeps walls to catch one, but it is worth it. The brushes last, Milady, they do.”

“Well, maybe you could borrow one from Morvran until you can acquire another squirrel, then.”

“I will ask him, Milady.”

“I hope he does, now take my hand and let us return to our time.”

“Yes, Milady.”

As they transferred from one time to another, the only difference between the two caves was a slight temperature variation.

“Thank you, Milady, for helping. I feel silly for losing such a vital part of my Charge duties.”

“Do not fret, Cradoc. I would rather help than to have seen you punished for such a small mistake.”

“Again, I thank you, Milady,” says Cradoc as he speeds back to the barracks, clutching the pouch close to himself. As she watched him race away and disappear into the trees, she couldn’t help thinking about the young man she had met on the other side, in another time. The range of emotions she had felt when she met the one called ‘Kenrich.’ Never before had she felt so at peace, so free, as she had in his presence. Her mind filled with joy and happiness as she remembered him. “I must return to that place by the Lake soon, and find this happiness again,” she said aloud.

CHAPTER SIXTEEN

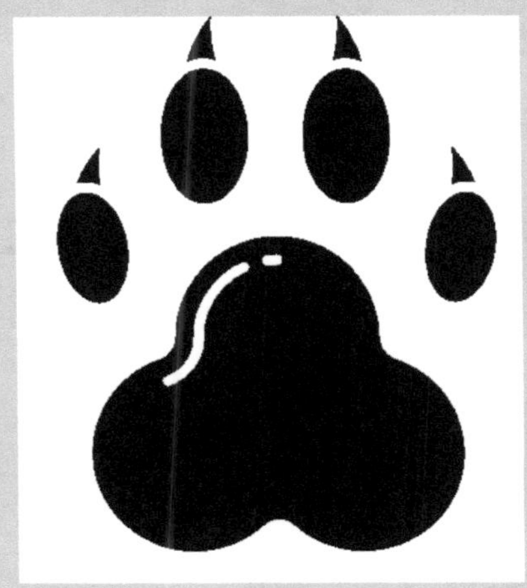

Griffin left the barn and ran up to his room. He rummaged through the tall stack of books he had piled up on the floor next to his desk till he found the one he was looking for, The Mabinogi. A book of legendary Welsh tales.

"Yes," he yelled loudly. Sitting on his bed he opened the book and went straight to the 'Four Branches of the Mabinogi.' The Second Branch was the 'Mabinogi of Branwen,' Griffin remembered the story now, she died of a broken heart. The name means 'White Raven' in Welsh.

"Griffin, are you okay?" said Amelia, "I heard you yelling."

"I'm okay, Mom, sorry!"

"Okay, but please stop the yelling. We can hear you from the kitchen."

"Will do, Mom."

She returned to the kitchen and to the cup of tea she had been enjoying, along with the company of Gavin and Charles.

"Boys got a set of lungs on him, Hun," said Gavin.

"Reminds me of someone else I know," Charles said with a smile.

"Yeah, you're right about that, Dad," Gavin said, blushing. "I sure wasn't the soft-spoken kind as a kid."

"Well, look who just stepped through the door. Where have you been this fine day, Ken?" asks Charles.

"I went up to Lake Percival, Grampa?"

"Why in God's good name would you do that? We don't know if that area is safe yet."

"I told him it was okay, Dad."

Charles turns and gives Gavin a stern look, "Why?"

"Its' okay, Grampa. Everything is fine up there," Ken couldn't hide his dopey smile.

Amelia picked up in the change in her eldest expression right away, smiling she asked, "Tell us why you're smiling like a Cheshire cat, Ken?"

Ken took the empty seat at the table and helped himself to a cup of tea. "I met the most beautiful girl at the throne just now. Her name was Branwen, and she is everything!" he dreamily looked off into the corner of the kitchen and his parents looked at each other in astonishment.

"Ken!" said his father, giving his arm a tug, "wake up, boy!"

They chuckled as Ken blushed bright red and stood up, forgetting his tea, "She was so amazing! I'd never felt like this before."

Amelia put her hand on Ken's arm, "Take a few minutes and breath, Ken. She must have been very special to have caused you this much distress."

Ken breathed, and then sat back down at the table. He picked up his now cold tea, sipping as he tried to get his blush under control. Charles looked a combination between mad and concerned, "What was she doing there, and where did she come from?" he asked accusingly.

Amelia looked across the table at Charles, "Charles, one question at a time, don't you see he has had a shock."

"Sorry, Amy."

Ken put his elbows on the table. "I honestly don't know where she came from, Grampa. Kay and I had been sitting on Grand Daddy when she sat up and started sniffing the air, that was when I smelled it."

Amelia refilled Ken's teacup and asked, "Is that when you saw her?"

"Kay was facing the west of the property when she started sniffing, so I looked over the back of Grand Daddy. She was hiding behind a big oak tree. At first, she wouldn't reveal herself to me, even though I called out. I could sense her fear, but she did step out and introduce herself."

"You could actually sense her fear?" asked Gavin.

"I guess so, Dad. She said her name was Branwen. I felt her need to be closer to me, but when she saw Kay, she stopped. I could feel her fear rising, getting stronger, and she said that she must go, or she would be missed. It didn't make much sense. She turned quickly and ran back into the trees. I called out, but she was already gone."

Sensing Ken's sadness, Amelia hugged him to her. "She ran to the west, you say?" asked Charles.

"Yea, Grampa. I didn't want her to go, and I was going to follow, but something inside me said not to follow."

"It's possible that she could be associated with the evil ones, or be one herself," says Charles.

"No way, not possible! She was so beautiful, and I felt so peaceful around her. It was like she was calmness and happiness all in one person. No way was she evil," says Ken.

"I'm sure that she is a fine young lady, but we have to be careful," Charles says, patting Ken's hand. "There's nothing in the west side of the lowlands. No shelter other than the line of caves, the Black Bear Caves, along the edge of the property. Not much use out there. It's filled with dry, barren lands, not even fit for grazing."

"Hardly the place a girl would want to hide out in. Maybe she is in trouble," says Amelia.

Griffin sat on the porch steps just outside the kitchen and listened in on the conversation between Ken and the parents. He took in all that Ken was saying about his encounter with Branwen, but what really piqued his curiosity was what Grampa said about the Black Bear Caves. He had never heard of any caves in the valley, and he figured now would be a good time to ask Grampa about it.

"Hi, everyone. What are you talking about? I heard Grampa say something about caves?" he tried for an innocent face, but his family knew him too well to fall for that.

"First things first, young man," Amelia said, frowning, "what's with all the yelling lately?"

"Sorry, Mom. I was playing with Owen on my tablet, and I just beat his war lord in battle. It was so exciting. So, I was on the porch stairs outside just now and heard something about a cave? I didn't know there were caves on the farm."

"That's were Grampa killed a black bear," says Ken.

"Cool, Grampa!" says Griffin.

"Well now, let's not get ahead of ourselves. I didn't kill the bear, or well I guess I did, but it was dying anyway. I just put it out of its misery," Charles says.

"Tell me, Grampa Charles, what happened?" asks Griffin.

"It was many years ago. I guess I was about the same age as Ken here. I was hunting deer south of Lake Percival and I came across a blood trail leading to the northwest. I followed it till I came to a narrow opening in the west wall of the valley."

"Did you go after it, Grampa, into the cave and everything?" eagerly asks Griffin. "Wasn't that dangerous, I mean, it was a wounded bear."

"Oh no, not then. I could hear it breathing. It was labored and then it grew quiet. I laid my crossbow behind me on the ground and, pulled out my dad's .38. Back then there were a lot more bears and mountain lions, so it was common to carry a side arm anytime you went into the back forest."

"Did you have to use the .38 on the bear, Grampa?" asks Griffin.

"Nope. I used my crossbow."

"But!" Gavin put a hand on his son's arms, "let gramps finish, son."

"It's not that complicated. The bear came out of the cave and walked right by me, paying me no mind. He was really in a bad way, but I still froze. I could have shot him right then, but the noise would have alerted every deer in the area. The bear went about twenty paces from me and just sat. I think it would have died eventually, but I didn't want to take the chance on it hurting anyone. So, I reached down and grabbed my crossbow, putting a bolt right in its chest. It dropped right away. I waited for any movement for about half an hour, but there wasn't any. It had died."

"What did you do with it after it had died, Grampa?"

"I skinned it and hung it on the barn, but it disappeared not long after. I still have its tooth though," says Charles.

"I still wonder who would have taken it," says Gavin.

"We may never know, but if we do, I can prove it belongs to me because I cut my initials on the inside of the skin, just below where my bolt penetrated it. I did find out that the folks two farms to the west of us shot a black bear that was mangling their gardens. It ran off and they followed a blood trail till it went into the forest. They never did find it. I'm pretty sure they're one and the same."

"Grampa Charles, can I see the tooth?" asks Griffin.

“Don’t you think Grampa’s story was enough for now, Griffin?” says Amelia.

“Oh, that’s no problem at all, Amy,” says Charles, “It’s right here on my necklace chain.” He reached inside his collar and pulled out a gold chain. The single item attached to it was a large bear tooth. He took the necklace off and handed it to Griffin.

“Wow, that’s so cool!” says Griffin, holding up the bear tooth and comparing it to the length of his own fingers.

“The gold chain was a gift from Aunt Josie. She took the tooth to a jeweler friend, and he mounted it on the chain for my birthday.”

Griffin gripped the tooth tightly. He could still feel the strength of the long dead bear through the tooth. “It’s beautiful Grampa.” He handed the chain back to Charles.

“Time to get back to work, everybody. Dad, you want to give me a hand with Oscar. Seems that old tractor is getting harder to start,” says Gavin.

“Might need a new starter then,” questions Charles.

They all got up from the table, ready for the day to be done, but heading out to finish the last of the evening chores before bed. Griffin got up from the table and headed to the front porch, with Ken close behind.

“Griff, wait up! I want to ask you something,” says Ken.

It was easy for Griffin to guess what his brother wanted to ask, since he was thinking the same thing. “Let me check the fence lines in the morning. I also want to check out the Black Bear Caves.”

“Sure, but I’m coming with you,” says Griffin, leaving no doubt that he was going to check those caves out too, with or without Ken.

CHAPTER SEVENTEEN

It was early the next morning when Branwen awoke to a turmoil out on the trail near her hut. She hurriedly dressed and stepped outside and was met by a nasty odor. She could see several Charges pulling a large wagon filled with animal dung along behind them, and down the narrow path toward the village.

One of the Charges saw Branwen standing at her gate and waved hello, "Morning, Milady. Sorry for the mess, but the mistress requires this for her garden of thorns."

She waved them on, not saying a word to them as they passed, but placing her hand over her nose to help block out the smell. She waited near her gate till the sickening odor had left before returning to her hut, but she slowed, feeling like she was being watched. From up the trail came Elder Meilyr. He was a tall, handsome man and his clothes fit him well. "Hello, Lady Branwen, how are you this fine morning?" he asked, smiling at her as he approached.

"Elder Meilyr," said Branwen, as she gave him a nod out of respect to his rank. She was keenly aware of his interest in her. Several times he had attempted to make advances toward her, but she was able to elude him every time. "What brings you out this way?"

"I have just been to the Well of Healing. Have you not heard?" he says, with a devilish smile on his lips.

"No, Elder Meilyr. What have I missed?"

"One of Elder Macsen's Charges was healed earlier this morning."

"Who was it? What did they do to deserve to be healed, Sir," she asked, glad that it wasn't Cradoc or one of his Charge since they were not under the control of Elder Macsen, but fear for the two conspirators from yesterday, Rhain and Gerallt, swept over her. She knew better than to express her concerns to openly in front of Elder Meilyr.

"Charge Gerallt was found to have been attempting a revolt on Elder Macsen's control this morning. When confronted, he stabbed Macsen!" he said heatedly, feeling quite roused by the audacity of a Charge to even attempt anything against an Elder.

"How is Elder Macsen?"

"He will survive, but his recovery will be lengthy."

"What of Charge Gerallt?"

“I have healed him at the Well. His spirit is now free of his treachery. You would have enjoyed his suffering, I’m sure, Milady Branwen,” he says, leering at her as he walked away. She held back her contempt for Meilyr, and his boastings. “Has the burning been performed?” she asks. Afraid of what his answer will be.

“That is why I am here, Lady Branwen. I made sure that Macsen’s Charges attended the Healing, as a warning to them. They are all waiting at the Well of Healing, waiting for you, Lady Branwen, to perform the Ritual of the Burning.” It was as she feared. She wasn’t the only one who could perform the ritual, but it was a way of making her see she was just as much as a prisoner in the Keep as the poor Charges.

“I will not be returning to the Well of Healing; my part is done. I have more important things that need my attention. I’m sure you can handle it alone.”

“Very well, Elder Meilyr. I will be there shortly,” she says. “Has the Mistress been informed?”

“Oh yes! It was the Mistress who informed me of Gerallt’s plans, but it seems I was not in time to prevent Macsen’s terrible attempted assassination.” Watching the vile man continue on down the path toward the outskirts of the village, she turns around and heads into her hut to prepare for her day.

She couldn’t begin to guess how the Mistress had learned of the plans so quickly, and she was suddenly very worried about her own fate, now that she knew the Mistress was aware. She had to have known that Meilyr could not have gotten to Macsen in time. She gathered the materials she would need for the Burning and left her hut for the Well of Healing within the Keeps walls. As she came upon the chamber that held the Well of Healing, she could see Elder Macsen’s Charges grouped together, quietly murmuring to each other.

“Good day, Milady,” grumbles Rhain. The rest of the Charges stand silently as she enters the chamber. She sees Gerallt’s body lying on the chamber floor, bodily fluids streaming off of him.

“There is nothing good about his day, Charge Rhain. I sincerely hope that you all have learned something from this senseless incident today.” She looks out at the assembled Charges with a grim set to her features. They all fell silent.

“Now carry this body, of a once fine Charge, to the Burning Stone.” She follows the Charges as they carry the body of their former friend and compatriot from the chamber, and out of the Keeps south entrance, just outside of the kitchens. They held the Burning Stone on a large mound, barren of any life, a large, flat stone at its peak.

She waited as the body had been lain on the stone, then she began to say the ritual that would burn the body and release any lingering spirits. “We burn this shell to rid it from our midst. Let the winds carry the ashes to the far away sea.” At that moment, she raised her arms and let loose the power from her hands. Gerallt’s body burst into flames.

The gathered Charges, with their heads bowed, crossed their arms and dropped to their knees. As they watched, the fire consumed the body until only ashes remained. As Branwen lowered her arms a breeze came from everywhere at once and carried the ashes from the stone to the sea. “Let us forget these ashes and remember the true spirit of Gerallt is among us still.”

She watched as the Charges stood and silently walked back into the Keep, leaving her alone at the Burning Stone. She turned and saw that Charge Rhain was till kneeling before the stone, silent tears coursing down his face.

“Rise Charge Rhain, the ritual is over now.”

“My sorrow runs deeper than that of the other Charges, Milady”

“You were good friends then?”

“Yes, that is true, Milady.”

“Then, why did he do such a terrible thing then, Rhain?”

“Milady, I…” Rhain was afraid to go on.

Branwen could guess at his feelings. “I know what has been going on within Macsen’s Charge. All the Elders have been having issues with their Charges since the Falls have been halted, but please be calm. I’m sure the Mistress is aware of your concerns and will prepare for change shortly.”

“Yes, Milady,” he says quietly, not believing that the Mistress cares about the welfare of the Charges. “I pray to the Gods that she will.”

“As do I. Now catch up with your Charge brothers now.”

He stood up and ran back toward the Keep. Branwen waited till he was out of sight and walked back into the Keep, her duties to her Mistress called. As she entered the Mistress’s chambers, she saw her sitting near the fire.

"Where did you go yesterday, Branwen?" asked the Mistress, still facing the fire. That caught her by surprise, normally she could come and go as she wished as long as Mistress did not need her. She had to think quickly, the truth was the only option she could see, the Mistress seemed to already know about her journey through the Fall yesterday.

"I was with Charge Cradoc, Mistress."

"And what, exactly, were you two doing?

"He had lost a pouch on his last Fall, that he needed for his duties and asked me to help him."

"Was the Charge able to reclaim their property?"

She hesitated for just a moment, but it was enough time for the Mistress to answer for her, "No need to tell me Branwen. I know you went to the location of Cradoc's last fall. What I want to know is why you had to keep this from me, to disobey me when I said there would be no further Falls."

Branwen dropped to her knees. "I'm so sorry, Mistress! I just wanted to help him. He is a good Charge. Please don't punish him too harshly. It was my idea to go, and I will take punishment, anything you wish."

The Mistress stood from her fire side chair and looked down at Branwen. The disobeying of her orders normally deserves the taking of an ear, but she paused when she saw the tears falling down the lovely face. "Rise, Branwen. There was a time I would have your ear, but you are what I need to keep myself in power. You have the gifts that I never had, and I have much planned for you and me, and I need your loveliness to help accomplish this," the Mistress said, running a long finger over Branwen's cheek.

Trembling in relief as well as disgust she cries out, "Oh, bless you, my Mistress."

"Now, for Cradoc. It was he who informed me of your Fall yesterday."

"I don't understand, Mistress?"

"He came to me with information of a revolt against Elder Macsen by a few of his Charges. When he told me where he had heard this, I questioned him on why he was in the chamber at that time. He told me right away of your plans. I immediately took his ear, impudent Charge, but spared his life since he informed me of the plans against Elder Macsen's life."

“Mistress, I met Elder Meilyr and he told me of Gerallt’s attempt on Elder Macsen’s life. I performed the Ritual of Burning not too long ago.”

“Yes, I ordered Meilyr to inform Macsen of this news, but unfortunately, he was too late. A shame, really.” Her tone informed Branwen that she wasn’t very sad over idea of a loss of a particularly vile Elder.

“Mistress, shouldn’t we start the Falls up again. Do you think this might relieve the tension within the Charges? I myself have witnessed the Elders becoming more, spirited, of late.”

The Mistress Morgana walked toward the fire and sat down in her chair, pulling the blanket around her robed form. “You may be right, Branwen. Although Macsen always has held and iron fist around his Charge, and at times I sensed he wanted more control over the way the Keep was run, than just his one Charge. I will call the Elders together tonight and inform them that Falls will commence again starting tomorrow.”

“Yes, Mistress.”

“One more thing, Branwen. When you and Cradoc were on your Fall, did you notice anything unusual? It was told to me by Morvran that he and Cradoc were scared away by an old man who seemed to be in control of the mist?”

“I saw nothing like that Mistress, nothing unusual,” she keeps silent about meeting Kenrich.

“Good. I’m sending Meilyr and a small group of Charges there tomorrow to take what was rightly fully mine.”

Branwen’s mind was full of racing thoughts as she stepped out for a breath of fresh air. She knew she had to return to Kenrich and warn him.

CHAPTER EIGHTEEN

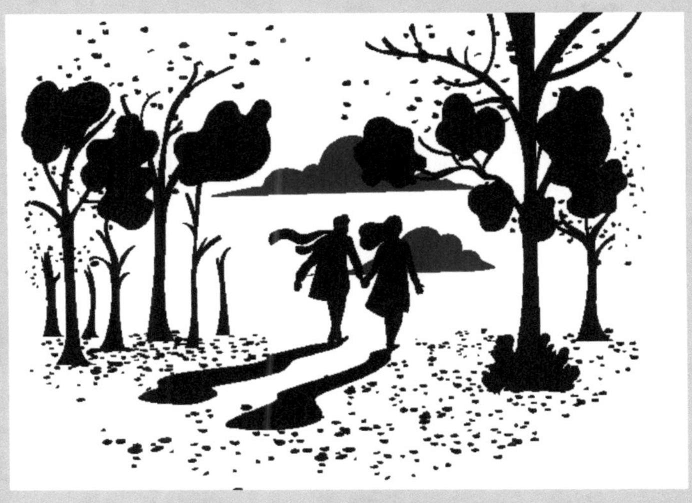

The dew hung heavy in the July morning air. Griffin wiped moisture from his hands after he slid the shed door open. He had been hoping that Ken would be there waiting, but there was no sign of him in the barn. Hearing movement behind him, he turns and sees Ken rushing up toward him. "What kept you? I could have been gone a long time ago."

"Sorry, Griff, had to help Dad and Grampa with Oscar. I think it's time they put it to rest," says Ken, walking into the barn.

"That's never gonna happen, Ken. You know how much Grampa loves that old tractor," he says, climbing into the passenger seat of the Panther next to Ken. Ken started the Panther's engine and they slowly moved out of the barn's doorway, driving up the lane between corn fields till he reached the pasture. They headed through the north gate and back into the Lake country, stopping only when they reached Grand Daddy. Griffin smiled to himself, knowing that the north gate now had its own red dragon protective symbol marked on it, which had surprised him at first. Why he didn't think about putting one on the gate sooner, he didn't know, but felt good about having one on their now.

Ken parked the Panther to the south of Grand Daddy and stepped inside. Facing west, he held out his arm and pointed. "See the big oak, Griff, that's where she was standing."

Griffin's newly enhanced senses could pick up a strange, but mild, aroma still clinging to the undergrowth as he stepped closer to Grand Daddy. "Did she run west into the forest, Ken."

"Yes, and we need to find her trail. I have to know who she is and why she was here."

"I thought Grampa said there was no place for anyone to go on this side of the valley?"

"That is what he said, but he also mentioned Black Bear Cave, and that's where we are going," says Ken.

"Do you know where it is located, then?"

"I've a pretty good idea, Griff. Looking west from the other side of Lake Percival, you can just see that the hills have dropped off leaving a line of cliffs visible through the treetops. It's not far from the stone wall, and I've been there many times."

"Have you ever seen a cave?"

"No, there's a lot of overgrowth on the walls, and besides, I wasn't looking for caves when I was hunting deer," explains Ken.

Griffin stepped around Grand Daddy and picked up another faint odor, but much less pleasing than before. He walked over to where he had flung the poachers pouch the day Grampa confronted the evil ones, but it was gone. Many times, since being accepted he had checked the pouch for any signs of a disturbance, but it had always been in the same spot. Checking all around, he found a brush on the ground. Holding it close he could still pick up a slightly musty odor coming from it. He quickly put it in his pants cargo pocket.

The boys searched the area for any sign that Branwen had left that they could follow but found nothing. They continued west toward the valley wall, following what looked to be a deer trail. After a few minutes of walking, Griffin stopped. His nose became filled with the most pleasant smell. "Ken, can you smell that?"

Ken was a few paces to his right when he too smelled something pleasing. "Yes, yes, I do. That's the same smell from yesterday."

Griffin could sense a presence nearby. "Wait, Ken," yelled out Griffin, "someone is coming." He pointed, "Someone is coming from that direction." Ken looked alarmed at Griff 's confidence, when he could sense no one approaching. "I'll explain later, Ken."

Ken knew who it must be and hurried down the trail, pushing in front of Griffin. "It's her, Griff. I know it!"

The boys stood there for several seconds, watching a woman come down the trail toward them. Ken was motionless, barely breathing. Her beauty filled his heart to bursting. "Branwen? That is your name? I got it right?"

She could feel his desire, his need, for her. A soft glow surrounded him, bringing out the color of his eyes. "Yes, Kenrich, it is me, Branwen," she smiled shyly at him.

They moved toward each other, not taking their eyes from one another. It was as if they were the only ones in the world at that moment. They knew a bond was forming that nothing could ever break. The spell was broken when she caught movement behind Ken and saw he wasn't alone, Griffin moved forward. Immediately, she dropped to her knees and hung her head. "Seeker, please forgive my ignorance!" she begged.

Ken and Griffin, both, were surprised by her sudden behavior. Ken could see that all of her attention was focused on Griffin, "Is she talking to you, Griff?"

Griffin stepped closer, "I believe she is."

"But Griff…"

"It's okay, Ken," said Griffin, "I'll fill you in later." Griffin looked down at Branwen, "I have no need to forgive you. If anything, I should be asking for your forgiveness. You have done nothing but bring happiness to my brother, and to the farm," says Griffin. He helps her to stand. She looked at him in astonishment. "I'm sorry. I never expected to meet a Seeker, and one so young too."

Griffin smiled up at her, "Yes, and I have never met an enchantress either, or one so beautiful."

"Your brother, Kenrich, has the gift of Love, Seeker," she turns to stare shyly into Ken's eyes. Both of them blush as their eyes meet.

"What brings you to our valley?" asks Ken.

"To warn you and your Blood!" she says.

"Warn?" says Ken, "Are we in danger?"

"They are coming tomorrow," cried Branwen, "to take back what the Mistress claims is rightfully hers."

"Who is your Mistress and what does she mean 'claim what is Her's'" asks Griffin.

"She goes by many names, Seeker Griffin. Her claim is to dominate over those families with a noble history."

"Is the shield with red chevrons hers, then?" asks Griffin.

"Yes, I'm afraid so. I'm afraid I have brought you a concern you will find hard to believe. I really must go now." Ken looked to Griff for help.

"Must you go so soon?" asks Griffin.

"Yes, Seeker," says Branwen, "before my Mistress misses me." She looks into Ken's eyes. "I will return soon, but first, you must warn you Blood of what is coming." She turned and ran back into the forest. Ken started to follow her when Griffin grabbed his arm, 'Let her go for now, Ken. We have to get home and warn them."

Ken reluctantly lets her go and follows Griffin back to the Panther. Once the engine is revving the urgency of what is coming tomorrow spurs him on, and they race across the pastures and fields back toward home.

CHAPTER NINETEEN

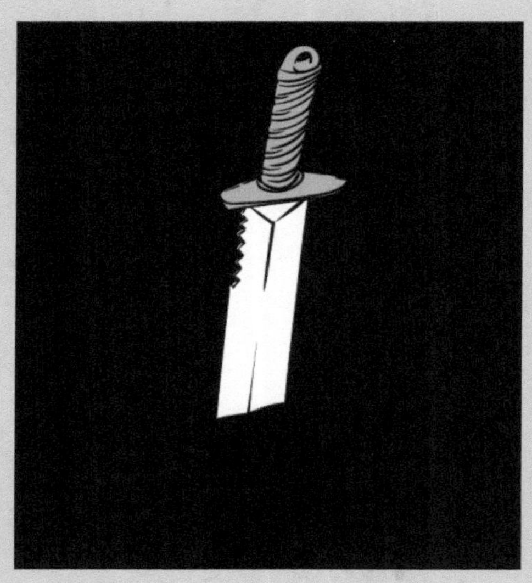

Mistress Morgana stood tall as her Elders bowed when she entered the meeting hall, with Branwen close behind her. "I have called this meeting to information you that the Falls will continue tomorrow." The Elders began to talk quietly amongst themselves. She raised her right hand, and the Elders became silent. "I will not tolerate your muttering while I am speaking!" All the Elders fell to their knees and bowed their heads.

"I see that you have grown impatient long enough, as have your Charges. It is time to continue the Falls. I will not tolerate the infighting any further, the attack upon Elder Macsen, was intolerable. Rise now and prepare your Charges." The Elders rose and bowed as they left the meeting hall. "Branwen, tell Elder Meilyr, I would have a word with him."

"Yes, my Mistress," she stepped from the meeting hall and approached the gathered Elders as they conversed among themselves. "Elder Meilyr, the Mistress would have a word with you."

"Yes, Milady," he leered at her as he walked back into the meeting hall. It was hard for Branwen to hide her distaste for the man. She stayed near the doorway after Elder Meilyr exited the corridor. Her heart started to race as she listened to their conversation.

Elder Meilyr bowed his head toward Mistress Morgana, "I am at your command, Mistress."

"Meilyr, you remember why I shut down the Falls?"

"Yes, my Mistress two of the Charges were confronted by a mist brought on by an old one of 'noble blood.'"

"Yes, Meilyr, Charges Morvran and Cradoc. I want you to return with them and punish this so called, 'noble blood.' Let them be made aware of who their master really is," she said, with glee.

"What if they call forth the Mist again, my Mistress?"

"Branwen will be among you. She has the power to protect against such conjuring."

"Very good, my Mistress. I will prepare my Charge." He bowed his head and left the meeting hall. He smiled when he passed Branwen in the corridor.

"Did you hear our conversation, Branwen?" asks Mistress Morgana. Branwen walks into the meeting hall and stands in front of her Mistress with her head bowed. "Yes, my Mistress, every word."

“Good! You will meet with Elder Meilyr and Fall to where a mist had frightened the Charges. Protect them from that mist should it appear again. The Elder and his Charge will deal with the ‘bloodline,’” she says, sweeping out of the meeting hall.

For the rest of the morning, Branwen had difficulty concentrating. Her thoughts were with Kenrich and the young Seeker, Griffin. How was she going to help them? She had to decide on her commitment to her Mistress. She owed her so much, and without her aide she would have been left for dead, but how could she continue knowing that such hatred was ever present within her Mistress. The love that Kenrich pulled from her heart had been hidden from her for too long. She felt it grow stronger each time they met, and she wanted to share it with every living thing. Finally, as she walked home, she made up her mind what she must do on the morrow.

As she neared her hut, she was startled by a voice coming from the shadows. “Milady Branwen, may I have a word?” Cradoc asks.

“Cradoc,” gasps Branwen in surprise, “what is wrong? You should be out with you Charge.”

“Forgive me, Milady, but I must warn you!” Cradoc’s pain was evident as he pressed his hand against his still bleeding bandage that covered what was left of his right ear.

“Cradoc! You’re in pain. Come with me and I’ll put a new dressing on it,” she said, pulling the small man behind her.

“Please, Milady, you must hear me out!” he said, trying to stop his forward march into the hut.

“I know about the Fall tomorrow. You don’t need to worry. I’ll be there to protect you from the Mist.”

“It’s not the Mist I’m worried about, Milady. Elder Meilyr has been ordered to make certain you do not return from the Fall,” he says, tears on his face.

“What!” she scanned the area to make sure no one was near them. “Who told you this?” her eyes were searching his face for any sign of a lie.

“I overheard Trystan, the Mistress’s guardsman, tell Elder Meilyr: ‘The Mistress wants you to make sure that Branwen does not return from the Fall,’” crying openly now, he gasps, trying to breathe through his hysteria.

“What did Elder Meilyr say?” she asked, bringing him a cup of tea and a biscuit.

“He wanted to know why, but Trystan knew not the answer.”

Branwen paused, thinking. “Cradoc,” whispered Branwen, “you must be very wary from now on, especially on tomorrow’s Fall. Trust no one, not even Morvran. Now come, let me clean that wound.” She could see that his wound had gotten infected, but she managed to clean it and apply a special lotion she had on hand for just such occasions. A fresh dressing in place, and he was on his way. She watched as he entered the forest across from her hut.

She knew it would be certain death if she were to confront her Mistress. Would Kenrich and his ‘noble blood’ give her safe passage into their world? She could no sleep as she lay on her cot, worried about what fate awaited her on the morrow.

CHAPTER TWENTY

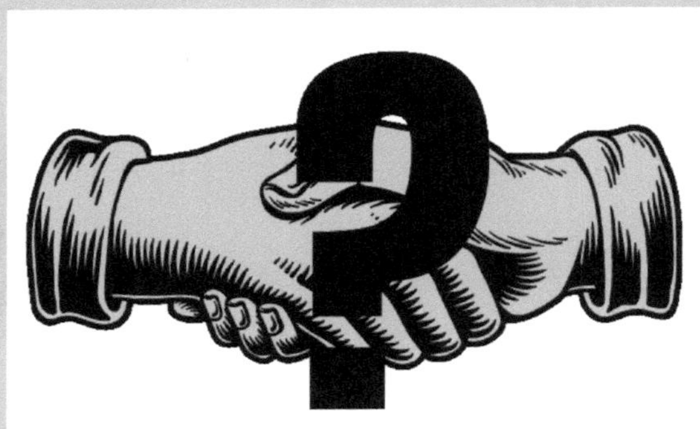

Ken and Griffin rushed back to the Panther. “I’ll drive Griff, you open the gate when we get to the pasture.”

“Wait, Ken!” he grabbed Ken’s arm, “there’s something I need to tell you.”

Ken pulled away from Griff’s grip, “What is going on, Griff? I’m not moving until you tell me what you’re up too.”

“I’m sorry, Ken, I should have told you sooner.”

“Told me what?”

“It’s going to sound crazy and you’re gonna think I’ve been playing on my tablet too much, but it was me who called the Mist that scared off the poachers.”

“What? You’re full of it, Griff, that was Grampa,” he exclaimed.

Griffin pointed at a bolder lying near Grand Daddy. It levitated off the ground as he raised his arm, and with a slight motion of his arm it splashed down into the Lake. “Do you believe me now?”

Ken’s mouth gaped like a fish as he stared at his little brother and then back at the Lake. “Uhm, yeah, I guess so, I think!”

“Follow me, there’s someone I want you to meet,” he says, stepping out toward the stream, Dee Run.

“Where are we going too, Griff?”

“The Bathing Stone, come on, hurry,” urges Griffin, running ahead.

“We don’t have time to sunbathe little brother, we have to get back and warn everybody!”

“We are not going up there to tan, Ken. You’ll just have to see for yourself. Now hurry up, big brother.” Griffin wasted no time getting to the glade that had the stone. He climbed right up on it and gestured for Ken to climb up as well.

“Come on up Ken and stand in the middle with me.”

Ken hesitated, not sure what his brother was playing at, but joined his brother atop the stone. “What are we doing, Griff?”

“Grab my hand, Ken. We are going on a Fall to the Stone of Return.”

“A fall? What kind of fall?” asked Ken.

Just then a mist formed around them, enveloping them in an opaque world one second and dissipating just as quickly, placing them on another Stone of Return. This time within a larger glade. One with a waterfall, and ancient trees towering above their heads, nearly blocking out the daylight. Griffin held onto Ken’s hand till he had steadied himself. “You Okay, Ken?”

“I think so,” he said, his eyes opening wide as he tried to take in his new surroundings. “Where are we, Griffin?”

“You are on the Stone of Return, young squire,” said a voice from a silhouette standing at the entrance to the glade.

“Master Seeker?” asked Griffin.

“Yes, my young Seeker, and this must be your brother, Kenrich, our newly accepted squire?” he said and stepped into the light shining down through the tree leaves. Ken stood motionless. His eyes fixed on the hooded man that Griff called the ‘Master Seeker.’ Griffin still had a hold of Ken’s hand as he led him down from the stone. “Ken, this is the Master Seeker, my friend.”

Ken was in awe as he held out his hand. “I, I am pleased to meet you, Sir. This is all a surprise to me.”

The Master Seeker shook Ken’s hand. “As am I to meet you, Kenrich. I feel you will bring good things to your blood.”

“Master Seeker, would you help me explain all this to Ken?” he asked.

“He already knows, Seeker Griffin. Your entry into the Mist has allowed his mind to be opened to the needs of your family and your bloodline. He will be a strong defender.”

Griffin looked at his brother, who was standing there with his chest puffed out, and back at the Master Seeker. “We have been warned the evil ones will come to our home to attack us tomorrow. We were warned that they plan on taking back what was rightfully theirs. We need your help!”

The Master Seeker put his hand on Griffin’s shoulder and looked into his eyes. “The Elders have told me of your troubles, young Seeker. Do not fear, for you will have your spirit to guide you. Now you must Fall home to tell your blood of the danger that is approaching,” he says as he guides them back toward the Stone of Return.

As the two boys stand upon the Stone of Return, their minds are trying to take in what the Master Seeker had said. Then they saw him raise his arms and shout 'Byth Heb' as the Mist engulfed them and sent them back to their time.

Ken fell forward onto his knees as he came to rest on the Bathing Stone. "I see why it's called a Fall."

"Ken, my senses are picking up all sorts of strange vibes. Do you feel them too?" Griffin asked as he was climbing down the Bathing Stone's sides.

"Yeah, Griff, I do. What does it mean?" he asked increasingly worried about his family.

"I believe we have visitors who would do us harm. I'm sorry you haven't the time to hone your skills Ken, but just follow your instincts and you'll do fine."

Ken jumped down from the stone and joined his brother. "We have to warn the family, Griff!"

Griffin held up his hand to stop Ken and scanned their surroundings, "If we have time, brother, but first we must stave off these evil ones. Come, let's hasten to Grand Daddy."

As they ran toward Lake Percival, Ken saw a change come over his 12-year-old brother. He was not acting like a child any longer, but as a man with a noble cause.

"I can smell them now. They come from the west, Griff. How can we defend against them? We have no weapons?" asks Ken.

"Ken, I have acquired many skills since I was accepted and became a Seeker. Our senses will guide us today, brother. Our sense of awareness is our strongest gift. They will not see us this day, but we will know their every movement." They stopped and dropped to their knees upon reaching the shore of Lake Percival.

"I can still sense movement to our west," says Ken.

"Yes, and they are spreading out," says Griffin, with his eyes closed, concentrating on the movement of many feet. "Some are going faster south and others north, I feel a strong force in the center. We will make our stand at Grand Daddy."

They hasten to Grand Daddy and take to their knees again, staying hidden within its protective walls. Peering over the back side to the west, they picked up the familiar stink of those who rarely bathe.

“The stink is getting stronger, Griff,” says Ken.

“Yes, they are very near.”

“What’ll we do? We’ve never had to kill anyone before!”

“I hope we can prevent any death this day, especially ours!” says Griffin. He puts his hand on Ken’s shoulder, and speaking lowly, says, “Stay very still, Ken. You will feel a slight vibration and then we will be invisible to them.”

Ken held his breath as he felt a quiver move through is body. His exposed skin had a tingle as if every hair was being gently moved around by an invisible breeze. They both stood as a voice came from the forest toward the west.

“Move onto the shore of that Lake,” yelled Meilyr. “We have to make this a foul pit that this bloodline will never again enjoy.”

Griffin felt the strength of the one who came closer. There were 12 evil ones in total, but only eleven were within his mind view as they came to the shoreline of Lake Percival. Meilyr stopped at the shoreline next to Grand Daddy. “I know you are here. I can feel your presence. I come here to rid this world, this time, of your bloodline’s existence. Leave now or face death upon our Burning Stone. Your powers do not frighten me!” he says grandly.

Griffin sensed this evil one searching for any sign of him and Ken. His words were hateful, and Griffin had heard enough. He dropped the invisibility, and stepped up onto the seat, just barely visible above the protection provided by Grand Daddy. “Turn and face your demise evil one!”

Meilyr turned and looked at Griffin who was standing on the throne. “You have no power over me,” spat Meilyr, raising his battle axe, “I will cut you to pieces and feed you to my Charge!”

Griffin held his ground, and said not a word, but raised both arms straight at Meilyr with palms exposed. In one quick motion he swung his arms out then then back toward Meilyr, slapping his palms together. A deafening sound thundered through the air, knocking Meilyr, and his Charge unconscious.

“Griff, what did you do?” asked Ken, coming around Grand Daddy.

Griffin cut him off. “I feel a familiar presence to our south. I believe it to be Branwen, and the lone evil one is with her. We must hurry Ken; she may be in danger!”

“What of these evil ones, Griff? Are we just gonna let them lie here?”

“They will remain like this for some time. When we know Branwen is safe, I shall return them back to whence they came.” As they stepped down from Grand Daddy, Griffin noticed a dark furry pelt clinging to Meilyr’s left shoulder. Remembering Grampa’s story about that Black Bear pelt that disappeared from the barn, he removed it and could just make out the initials ‘CMD’ carved into the lining of the hide next to a small slit, barely half an inch in length.

“What is it, Griff?”

“I believe we have found the thief who tole Grampa Charles’s Bear pelt.” The smell coming off the pelt was repugnant, and Griff wrinkled his nose in distaste. He waved his hand over the pelt, and, in an instant, the smell was gone.

“I can feel Branwen!” says Ken, running past Griffin.

“Wait, Ken! There’s still the other evil one with her, be careful.”

“Then you better keep up,” yelled Ken, “cause I’m not stopping.”

The ran to the south of Lake Percival and found Branwen crouching over a body. She heard them approaching and stood as they came into view. “Oh, Kenrich, and Seeker Griffin, I’m so glad you’re okay!” she reached out and hugged them both, tightly.

“Why is there an evil one with you?” asked Ken.

“This is Cradoc, a friend. He wants to leave the hatred he has had to endure and live in peace here, with you. Can you help him?” she asks.

Griffin knelt next to Cradoc. “He will be okay. I invoked a sleeping spell over the entire group. Their leader was about to poison the Lake.”

Ken put a hand on Branwen’s shoulder, “Are you Okay? Griffin’s spell didn’t harm you, did it?”

Their hands joined as she stood, and then they wrapped their arms around each other. “I am fine, and I sensed a change in you ‘Squire Kenrich,’” she smiled up at him brightly, giving his cheek a kiss. “A very pleasing change, I will say.” Ken, blushing furiously, smiled at her.

Griffin stood and looked down at Cradoc. “He is carrying the pouch I found at Grand Daddy.”

"Yes, Seeker, he is one that saw the Mist that day. He is a good person, truly. It was when we returned to find his missing pouch that Ken and I met."

Ken sniffed the air. "He no long smells rank. How is that?"

"I have a spell that protects me from their vile smell. All they really need is a good bath, of which they rarely get to partake, as you have experienced yourself. I have given Cradoc a cleansing spell, and he should no longer smell or be filthy."

Suddenly, there came a frantic call from the brush. "Seeker Griffin, we need your help!" Squire Grigor appeared, gasping for air.

"Squire Grigor, what are you doing here?" asks Griffin.

"Andras and I have been ordered to watch over you and Squire Kenrich and provide what aid we can. The Elders have informed the Master Seeker that you may need our aid sooner rather than later," he said, "they have upped their timetable and are here sooner than was thought. There is another one of the evil ones approaching your Lake, Seeker Griffin. We know this Charge to be led by one called Elder Macsen. He is a foul person and will destroy all your blood. Please come!" begged Squire Grigor, "Andras is watching them even now. If they spot him, they will kill him instantly."

Griffin turned to Ken and Branwen. "I must go, but you stay and protect Branwen and Cradoc, Ken."

"No! Griff! I can't let you go alone," Ken shouts after Griffin as he starts to run down the pathway toward the Lake.

"But…!"

Branwen grasps his arm tightly, "Macsen is very evil. He will not hesitate in killing all of your family. Kenrich will protect you. I have powers that will ensure our safety here, now go!" she turned and embraced Kenrich. "Take this," she says, handing him a sword with a long dark blade. "It will serve you well. Now be off with you!" She watches them as the run down the path, following Squire Grigor.

Ken looked back and waved as he vanished into the dark shadows of the forest. The trio ran north along the west bank of Lake Percival as Squire Grigor explained their dilemma. "Andras knows of Macsen through his many encounters with the evil ones. He is the most evil of them all. Andras wants you to know that Macsen will awaken that first Charge you encountered. You must make every effort to stop him, Seeker Griffin, even if their death is the only course to take."

“Listen,” says Griffin, “can you hear the shouting?”

“I hear it, Griff. It comes from near Grand Daddy, but I can’t tell what is being said,” says Ken.

Grigor cups his hand behind his ears and listens hard. “It is Macsen wanting to wake them from their deep sleep! We must hurry!” As they come closer, the shouts turn into understandable words. “Rise up you fools!” bellows Macsen. “Or your Mistress will have your ears. Let’s bleed this bloodline dry once and for all!”

CHAPTER TWENTY ONE

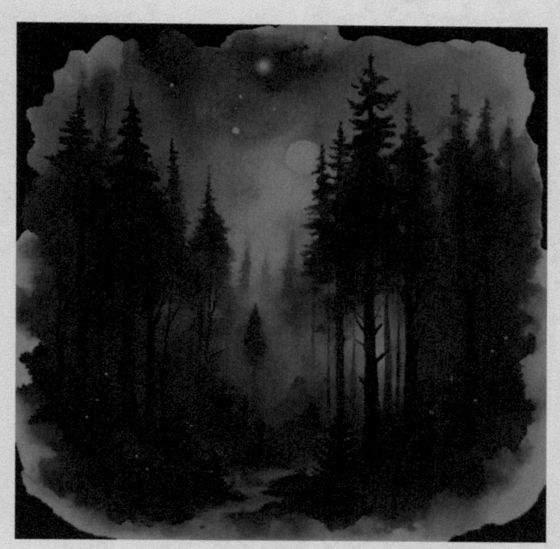

Gavin and Amelia were having their noon tea at the kitchen table when a breeze rushed through the screen door that led to the back porch. Gavin was sipping from his cup as the warm air touched his face and he froze, cup halfway to his lips.

Amelia noticed his sudden stillness, "What is it, Sweetheart? Are you Okay?"

Slowly, he lowered his cup, placing it back down onto its saucer. "Did you feel that warm breeze just now?"

"Yes, I did. It's a bit too early in the day to be that warm yet."

"It sure is, and I've never had a breeze whisper in my ear before, either" he said, standing quickly to his feet.

Amelia wasn't surprised by his actions. The whole family had been acting strangely since Charles told his story about history of the Defaid family bloodline. "What is it, Gavin? What did it say?"

"It was like a soft whisper in my ear. I heard two words, Byth Heb."

"Why those words? We know they say, 'Never Without,' but what are they really telling you?" she asked, having risen and was peering out the window above the kitchen sink. "Gavin, Charles is on Oscar, and he's coming this way!" Gavin and Amelia went onto the back porch as Charles pulled up near the house.

"Where you off to, Dad?"

"I got a strange feeling a couple minutes ago, Son."

"So did I, Dad. I think the boys need our help."

"Just what I was thinking. Get our crossbows and hop on, we're going up to Grand Daddy."

Gavin quickly gathered up their bows and quivers. Kissing Amelia's cheek and giving her a hug he asks, "You going to be, okay?"

"I'm locking up the house and Kay and I will stay inside until I hear from you, and don't worry, my old 12 gauge will be close by."

"That's my girl!" he says. He waved at her as Charles drove Oscar away. The ride to the north gate was a bumpy one as Charles wasted no time and pushed the tractor to its limits.

As the tractor came to a stop, Gavin jumped down to open the gate. "Wait, Gavin!" yelled Charles, who stepped down from Oscar. "It's Griffin!"

"What do you mean dad, is he okay?"

"It was Griffin who called the Mist that scared off the poachers."

"How do you know this, Dad."

"I felt his strength just now. He has the bloodline's gift of special powers."

"Then we must hurry."

"No, Gavin! We must go on foot. Oscar's engine noise will alert any evil ones of our approach."

A few minutes later as they approached Lake Percival's south shoreline, Gavin stopped short. "Did you hear someone shouting?"

"Yes, I did, and it wasn't a pleasant sound, but I also sense we are getting closer to Griffin."

"So do I, Dad, look," he said, pointing toward the north, "I see Ken, and there's Griffin. Who is that with them, though?"

CHAPTER TWENTY TWO

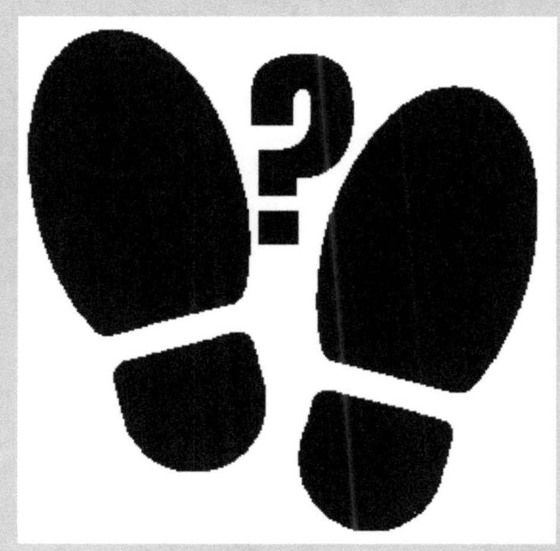

Griffin watched as one by one the evil ones began to rise from their deep sleep. Most were dazed and found it difficult to stand, while others popped up ready for action.

"Grigor, can we join Andras? I must get closer if I am to use my powers at full strength."

"Yes, but we must be as silent as a falling leaf!" he says.

"Wait! I hear movement from behind us," warns Ken. All three turn and see Gavin and Charles approaching through the tall grasses and tree trunks.

"What are you two doing here?" asks Ken.

"We were told you needed our help," offers Charles.

"But how?" asks Griffin, perplexed at their sudden appearance.

"Your plea for help came to us on the wind. Now be quiet and let's continue on," says Charles.

As Griffin looked at them with pride, he felt his powers strengthen. He now knows that the love a family shares is the strongest power ever.

"Come, Seeker Griffin," says Grigor, "we must join with Andras."

As they join up with Andras, and introductions given, Griffin could see that most all of the Charges had gained back what awareness they had and were on their feet already. The Elder that brought the first Charge was standing near Grand Daddy, patting himself down, looking for the missing bear pelt. Another evil one, larger, whom he reasoned as another Elder, was standing near him.

Andras put a finger to his lips as they approached. When Griffin stopped at his side he leaned over to whisper in Griffin's ear, "The larger of the two is Macsen. We must stop him at all costs!"

"Sorcerer," cried out Macsen, "I know you are here. Show yourself, coward."

Charles rose from his cover with his crossbow directed at Macsen. "You will leave now or face your death, evil one!"

Suddenly, a cry was heard as the forest came alive with the screams of the many charging Charges. "Death to the blood!" They rushed toward Charles with hate in their eyes. One was too fast and got near Charles. He lifted his battle axe to deal a deadly blow when Ken came up beside them, and using Branwen's sword, struck

him down with a high slash. The wolf howl it made as it cut into the air echoed through the forest, stunning the Charges momentarily, which gave Griffin time to evoke a protective shield over his team.

Macsen approached the small group of defenders, pulling a sword from its sheath with a bright red glow emanating from its blade. "There are no powers that will protect you from this!" he cried, "my Mistress has lent me her weapon. It will not fail in your death, retched filth!"

The gathering Charges stopped, screaming in fear as the Mist gathered onto the Lake surface. When it reached the shoreline, it came to a rest near Grand Daddy. A figure, clad in chainmail and armor, appeared brandishing a sword with a blinding white glow.

As Macsen drew back to strike at Charles, his weapons red glow vanished as the blade turned to ash, drifting away with the breeze over Lake Percival. Surprised, he looked at his empty, gloved hands. Silence swept through the valley as the Charges kneeled and bowed their heads, as did Meilyr.

"Get to your feet you gutless worms!" yelled Macsen, "or I will remove your manhood!"

The armored warrior held his weapon at the ready. "There will be but one manhood lost this day, Elder Macsen!"

Macsen's hatred turned to fear as he heard his name come from the stalwart warrior standing over him. He looked out over the Charges he had just threatened and felt their hatred of him.

"You and your kind will leave, never to return here!" Then the warrior looked at Meilyr. "Take these blood-soaked Charges and this loud-mouthed coward, Macsen, back from where you came and heal your souls. Tell your Mistress, this is our blood, and she will never come here to harm or deface ever again."

Meilyr stood and bowed his head. "Yes, Milord. By your leave, Sire."

"Begone with you, now!" said the warrior.

Meilyr grabbed Macsen's arm and led him away. The Charges stood and bowed as they backed away and then turned and ran. Within seconds they had vanished back into the shadows.

The armored warrior then turned and faced the defenders. His red cape, flowing

in the wind, covered his torso till it dropped away exposing the Red Dragon emblazoned on his armored chest plate. He held up his arm with palm open, "Byth Heb," he says, turning away as the Mist returned, and the warrior was gone.

"Seeker Griffin, will you not see to your family, now?" asks Andras, "Grigor and I will stay here till we are certain all evil ones have left."

Griffin couldn't believe what he had just witnessed. Ken saving his Grampa from an evil one, and the armored warrior stepping from the Mist. He was confused and turned to his Grampa, then to his father for guidance.

"Stay with them, Son," says Gavin, "they may need your help."

"But Mom."

"Your mother is fine, young Seeker Griffin," his Grampa smiles and gives him a hug, which he gratefully returns. He looks at his Grampa in amazement, "Yes, my boy, we know it was you who called the Mist that day."

"We have the same blood, Son," says Gavin, "we could feel your strength when you put down those evil ones."

"Seeker Griffin, let us enter the forest and follow their trail. There may be stragglers," says Andras,

Griffin and the two Squires headed west following a blood trail in the trampled brush grass. As they entered the forest, Griffin turned and waved, a large smile taking up his whole face.

"Ken, will you see to Branwen and Cradoc? They will need your help," says Gavin.

"I should go look after Griff."

"No son, his powers will protect him. You must see to the others now." Gavin put his arm around Ken, "I'm so proud of you, Kenrich, you saved your Grampa from that evil one."

"Thank you, Kenrich! He would have had me if it wasn't for you. Where did you get that sword from anyway? I know our family has never handed down such a weapon."

"Branwen gave this to me," he said, brandishing the sword so his father and grandfather could look more closely at it.

"She has done well for you, Ken," says his father.

"She has my heart, Dad," Ken says, stepping off and heading south along Lake Percival.

CHAPTER TWENTY THREE

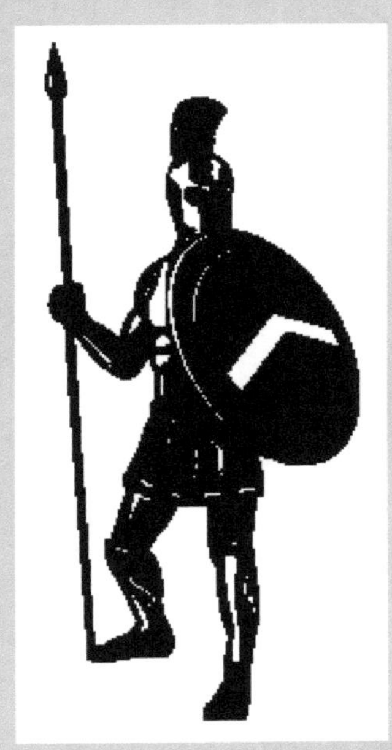

Grigor took the lead when entering the forest. "This must be the blood of the evil one that Squire Kenrich put down."

"I believe it will lead us to their entry point," says Andras.

"He's not dead yet!" says Griffin, catching up with them, holding up his arms.

Both squires freeze in their tracks to scan their surroundings. In the distance they hear loud screams and something thrashing through the underbrush. As the sound comes closer, they are able to see the tall brush being swept aside. Griffin quickly places a protective shield around them.

Through the brush explodes a huge black bear, holding the lifeless body of an evil one, which Kenrich prevented from attacking his Grampa. It paid them no heed, due to the shield, as it ran past.

"I do believe we have been spared any conflict from that evil one in the future," says Andras, "am I correct, Seeker Griffin?"

Griffin couldn't hold back a huge smile. He knew Andras was aware that it was his spell that had brought on the black bear.

"That was the biggest bear I've ever seen," said a wide-eyes Grigor. "Are all bears here so large?"

"I don't believe so, my young Squire. You can thank your young Seeker for that save."

"I believe I know where this trail will lead us. My Grampa calls it, Black Bear Cave. We have to close it off so they will never be able to use it again to gain access to this timeline," says Griffin.

They followed the trail of blood, picking up items dropped by the Charges as they fled. Coming to a stop next to a large oak tree, they could see the entrance to the cave in sight. The normally invisible entrance was now wide open due to the many bodies moving through it.

"This is where the evil one was waiting to ambush us," says Andras, "and you can see where there was a bit of a struggle when the bear attacked and drug him off."

"The cave is just ahead, and I don't sense anyone near," says Griffin, "but let's be careful when we enter."

Upon entering, Grigor felt the coldness of the rock surrounding him. The area had the reek of many unwashed bodies, a foul stench.

“Maybe we should leave here, Seeker,” says Andras.

Griffin held up his arm and, in his hand, appeared a torch. The cave lit up and filled with warmth and light. “It will get better, Grigor. The stink is from the evil ones, but soon it will be gone.”

Their trek took them deeper into the cave than was expected, but finally they had to stop. A wall of stone was blocking any further progress forward, it seemed like they had reached the end of the cave.

“Let’s get out of here,” says Griffin, ‘and seal this cave forever.”

“What do we do with these things? They serve no good purpose for us,” asks Grigor, holding up several bolts and a large battle axe.

“Leave them, Grigor,” says Griffin, “we want none of their trash.”

Griffin still held the torch upon their exit. After a few yards, he turned and tossed it back into the cave. Flames engulfed the interior and Griffin faced the cave opening. Raising his arms he yelled out: “let these flames consume any who enter with an evil heart!”

“I believe, Seeker, your homeland is clear of those who would do harm to your bloodline,” says Andras.

“Yes, I sense no threats toward my family now.”

“What of that huge black bear? It isn’t safe for anyone to venture into this valley with such a huge beast around,” says Grigor.

“Do not worry, Grigor,” says Griffin, with a smile, “when his meal is finished, he will return to his natural state.”

“Which is, Seeker?”

“A raccoon, Grigor,” says Griffin, chuckling, “there are several to pick from, but I chose the one nearest to the evil one. Do not worry about the raccoon, he will remember nothing of his adventure.”

Andras faced the bench within Grand Daddy as they gathered back at the beach by the lakeshore. “I see you have added the Welsh Dragon to your grandfather’s throne.”

"Yes, I did, and how do you know about Grand Daddy?"

"There are many things that we know of your bloodline, Seeker Griffin."

"I thought I was given all that knowledge by the Master Seeker?"

"He gives only what he has the right to give. That what you are wanting to know of your bloodline shall be passed on to you by the Elders."

"Why can't you tell me Andras? You seem to know much of my ancestors."

"A Squire learns many things along his journey and the most important is doing his duties to his utmost, with his eyes and ears open and his mouth shut. It is not my place to pass that story onto you, only an Elder has that right."

All three sat on Grand Daddy's bench and gazed out over Lake Percival in silence till a familiar voice could be heard.

"Hey, Griff!" shouted Ken, running up to Grand Daddy. "Is everything Okay?" Branwen approached the great tree stump from Ken's right.

Beside Branwen was Cradoc. She was holding the small man's hand. His clothing was now clean but torn and patched from years of use. Andras and Grigor stood and raised their crossbows, aiming at Cradoc's heart.

"No worries, Squires," says Ken, gesturing toward his two companions, "they are our friends."

Griffin stepped down from Grand Daddy and made introductions. "This is Branwen, Squires, she was the handmaiden of Mistress Morgana, but her heart it true. At her side is Cradoc a former Charge, now our guest. Both want to leave the evil ones and be free, both within their heart and soul."

"Seeker Griffin," says Andras, "Grigor and I will take the one called Cradoc back with us to the Stone of Return. The Master Seeker will have to decide if he is worthy to remain in our world, but you and Squire Kenrich should escort Branwen. I sense she has powers you should be aware of."

"You are correct, Andras," says Griffin, "she does have powers, and we will keep an eye on her."

"Thank you, Seeker Griffin. We shall see you at the Bathing Stone."

Griffin watched as the two squires escorted Cradoc along the Dee Run toward the Bathing Stone. "Griff, why did you say that? She's no threat to us!" says an annoyed Ken.

"I know that!" Griffin snapped at Ken. "What do you think the Master Seeker would do to her if those two Squires told him we weren't concerned about her powers?"

"Griffin is correct, Kenrich," says Branwen, "I must prove myself worthy of remaining here with you."

Ken looked at his brother, "I'm sorry, Griff, I don't mean anything by it."

"It's okay, Ken. Now, let's get to the Bathing Stone. We shouldn't be too far behind the others."

"Wait, Griff!" says Ken, "What about everyone else back home? Shouldn't we make sure they are okay before anything else?"

"They will be fine, Ken. I can sense their happiness, especially Grampa and Dad's returning home on the Panther. Their joy lifts my spirits. I'm sorry for not telling you sooner."

"No problem, Griff. You have been pretty busy today."

They walk to the Bathing stone, unhindered, and it gave Griffin time to take in Branwen's and Ken's feeling for one another. Being only a 12-year-old, he still thought it was gross, but he appreciated how happy his brother seemed. He jumped up onto the Bathing Stone and the others followed.

"I'm afraid, Ken," says Branwen, holding Ken's hand tight, "the Master Seeker may not accept me!"

"Your heart is pure, my Branwen. How can he not accept you?"

Griffin put her free hand into his, "You have nothing to fear, my friend."

Seconds later they were standing on the Stone of Return on the other side. It took a bit of adjustment, but when their eyes cleared, they saw a figure standing in front of them.

"Master Seeker!"

"Welcome, Seeker Griffin, Squire Kenrich. Squire Andreas has told me of your victory over Mistress Morgana's Charges. Well done, but why have you brought this evil woman here?"

"Master Seeker, this is Branwen. Her heart is pure, and she wishes to leave the service of her evil Mistress Morgana," pleaded Ken.

The Master Seeker studied the beautiful young woman standing before him. Griffin and Ken stayed at her side on the Stone of Return till they were told to step away. "Seeker Griffin and Squire Kenrich come stand next to me. Branwen, you will stay where you are, and the Stone will tell us if you heart is true or not."

"But, Master Seeker, I wish to be with her. What if she stumbles and falls?" asks Ken.

"If she is to be accepted, she must stand alone on the Stone. She has been influenced by an evil woman, an evil enchantress. That alone is enough to have her thrown from the Stone, but if her heart is pure, as you say, then she will be accepted."

Ken looked into eyes of the woman who had taken a hold of his heart. His eyes filled with tears as he watched her face contort in fear. Then the Mist engulfed her. Her body shook and swayed side to side. She tried to yell out, but was unable to make a sound, her face filled with abject fear. For a moment it looked as if she would fall, but then her body became still, her eyes closed, and her head tilted foreword. She stood motionless for some time, held within the Mist, then the Mist cleared around her. A ray of light shone from above surrounding her. She raised her head and with a huge smile yelled, "I'm free!"

Ken ran onto the stone, and they embraced and kissed. "You have been accepted! I knew you would be!"

"Master Seeker was Cradoc accepted?" asks Branwen.

"He was, but he is frail. The Squires took him to their hut and there they will look after him."

Griffin stepped near them and asked, "Will Branwen and Cradoc be able to return to our world, Master Seeker?"

"Branwen will be able to Fall whenever she wishes, but I'm afraid Cradoc will be with us forever. He hasn't the will to defend against evil ones any longer, he has earned his rest amongst us here," says the Master Seeker,

"May I take her to see him, Master Seeker?" asks Ken.

"Of course, Squire Kenrich, just follow the path after leaving the canyon. There hut is closest to the path."

"Thank you, Master Seeker," says Ken, with a bow of his head.

"Now, take Milady's hand and walk with her into this cool stream of water. It will refresh you both. Seeker Griffin, would you stay, I want a word with you."

"Yes, Master Seeker," says Griffin, watching as Ken and Branwen walked through the stream's waters and out of the canyon.

"I sense you have many questions my young Seeker," says the Master Seeker.

"I do, Master. Who was that warrior who came through the Mist to aid us?"

"You can ask him that question yourself," says the Master Seeker, "look to the Stone of Return."

Griffin looks up at the Stone as the warrior steps down. "My Liege, "says the Master Seeker, "this is Seeker Griffin Defaid. He is one of the defenders you have helped today."

Griffin bowed his head, "My Liege, you saved us today. I am in your debt."

"Welcome to the Isle of Apple Trees, Seeker Griffin Defaid. I commend you for your great courage on the field of battle today."

"Thank you, Sire."

"The young Seeker has questions only you can answer, my Liege," says the Master Seeker.

"Oh, does he now?" the warrior looks upon Griffin and with a smile says, "ask then, Seeker Defaid."

Griffin looked up into the eyes of the warrior. "Sire, I heard you tell the evil ones to tell their Mistress that our blood was yours and hers. Are we all the same blood, Sire?"

"Yes, we are of the same blood," the warrior reached out to Griffin and placed a gloved hand onto his shoulder, "You, I, and the Mistress Morgana are of the Pendragon bloodline, young Griffin."

Griffin could barely breathe. He knew that name from his heraldry studies. "May I ask, Sire? What is your name?"

"My name is Arthur."